MW01488541

The Blended Family Survival Guide

On Getting Married With Children
(yours or somebody else's!)

Brandi Mitchell

KORIS PUBLISHING

This book includes information gathered from many personal experiences. It is published for general reference and is not intended to be a substitute for independent verification by readers when necessary and appropriate. The book is sold with the understanding that neither the author nor publisher is engaged in rendering legal, or psychological advice. The publisher and author disclaim any personal liability, directly or indirectly, for advice or information presented within. Although the author and publisher have prepared this manuscript with utmost care and diligence and have made every effort to ensure the accuracy and completeness of the information contained within, we assume no responsibility for errors, inaccuracies, omissions or inconsistencies.

18 Years: The Blended Family Survival Guide
on Getting Married With Children Yours or Somebody Else's!

ISBN -13: 978-0-615-33461-5
ISBN – 10: 0-615-33461-X
Copyright 2010 by Brandi Mitchell
5080 Magnolia Walk
Roswell, Georgia 30075

Published by Koris Publishing LLC
P.O. Box 1151
Roswell, Georgia 30077

Printed in the United States of America.
All rights reserved under International Copyright Law.
Cover Designed By Shawn Meekins, Pennie Rainer, Jamour Chames
Interior Design and Layout By El Gee Artista
Font: Adobe Caslon Pro

QUANTITY DISCOUNTS ARE AVAILABLE TO YOUR COMPANY, EDUCATIONAL INSTITUTION, OR CHURCH

For reselling, educational purposes, counseling groups, subscription incentives, gifts, or fundraising campaigns

For more information, please contact the publisher at
Koris Publishing LLC P.O. Box 1151 Roswell, GA 30077
info@theblendedfamilysurvivalguide.com

DEDICATION

My source of strength and hope is in Christ alone.
Thank You Lord

To my parents Shirley & Don Hennings
and my grandparents Annie & Robert Morris
who loved and cared for me unselfishly
to make me the woman which became the wife of Curtis,
and mother of Kory, Brannen, and Curtis.
May your dreams be realized through me.

To My Four Guys
My husband Curtis, my supporter,
best friend, and the love of my life.
Kory, who brings us unimaginable joy,
and Brannen & Curtis for their sweet spirits.

Acknowledgments

I would like to take the time to thank all of the people who helped in the production of The Blended Family Survival Guide. The graphic artists: Shawn Meekins, Pennie Rainer, and Jamour Chames; Cortney Ball: for setting the atmosphere for me to write and to pour out onto the pages of this book; Tiffany Williams for being the "ram in the bush"; Tracey Baker-Simmons & Wanda Shelley for providing examples of how to do business, raise a family, and have integrity; Linda Davis for being a great mentor; Pastors Reginald & Kelly Lane and the Dunamis Outreach Ministries Family- for years of spiritual guidance and teaching me how to have an intimate relationship with God; Pastor Tyrone Temple: our premarital counselor who helped to provide the foundation for a strong marriage, which allowed us to plan for the success of our marriage; Donielle and Kevin Brown who were our blended family partners in the journey; and all of the friends, family, and well wishers who offered encouraging words and support.

Table of Contents

The Responsibility of Raising Children Other Than Those You
Birth

Time Shared

Being an Instant Parent, Your New Role and Responsibility

Factors to Consider with Your Spouse's Children

Children May Feel Disloyal

Your Life Has to Be Flexible

Emotional Availability

Giving Yourself a Permission Slip to Have Natural Feelings of
Jealousy and Insecurity

Conflict May Be Inevitable, So Care for Your Emotional Stability

Double Your Pleasure, Double Your Fun: When There are Multiple
Baby Mama's/Daddies

Being Understanding and UNSELFISH, Without LOSING
YOURSELF

It's All In How You Deal with the Conflict

Do You Care What Image You Are Portraying?

Honestly Identifying the Potential Conflicts

What and Who Causes the Conflict?

Conflict Between the Biological Parents

Conflict Initiated By the Ex

Conflict From the New Spouse

Anticipating Conflict

When Does the Conflict Occur?

What Are Some of the Triggers for Conflict?

Responding to Conflict By Role

For the Non-Custodial Parent Who Is Married

The Spouse

Some Quick Tips For Spouses

Some Tips For the Ex

Defining and Supporting the New Roles

Creating Blended Family Fun

Helpful Blended Family Tips

PART THREE: MOVING ON, GROWING UP, REALIZING WE'RE ALL IN THIS TOGETHER

Introduction

When Prince Charming found me, glass slipper in hand, we vowed our love to each other for eternity, as he whisked me off to Blendedville to live happily ever after. What I didn't expect, on the way to my not-so-new castle, was that we would pick up two, little adorable travelers that would go on the journey with us! Oh, and by the way, did I mention that my carriage had to stop to pick up my little travelers at two different houses? Now, a young princess in my new blended world, I had no map or compass to guide me through the blended journey, nor had I realized the true effect my ready-made family would have on my own marriage and future children.

Yes, I lived in a town called Blendedville, and my street's name was Reality – as I received real, on the job training, and we all made mistakes that turned into life lessons along the way.

I wrote this book because I saw so many people moving or headed to Blendedville, all looking for answers on how to live in their new world too!

In fact statistics show that ...

- 50 percent of all Americans are involved in some type of blended or stepfamily relationship which is about 75 million Americans.

- 30 million children under the age of 13 are currently living with one biological parent and that parent's current partner.

- In fact, everyday approximately 1300 new stepfamilies are formed in the US.

While in the middle of a tough time in my own blended family, it occurred to me that there needed to be a guide to provide people with solutions that were trying to live, thrive, and more so, survive, in a blended family. I always felt, "If only people knew what to expect on the journey". "If only I could tell them what was behind door #1, 2, 3, and 4!" I now know that my experiences in my blended family, both in my marriage and throughout my childhood, will help the millions of us today living life "blended."

The Blended Family Survival Guide is broken down into three parts to assist you in understanding, navigating, and finding solutions in blended family life:

Part One - Truth & Consequences, This section is the reality check for those who have children prior to marriage, and covers where the child lives, child support, visitation, and baby mama/baby daddy drama. In part one, we will take a close look at the baby mama/baby daddy history, it's influences, and the entire movement. This segment provides real-life scenarios with a level of transparency that has yet to be demonstrated in most books that attempt to cover blended family living.

Part Two - Getting Married with Children, This section meets the reader at the crossroad of going from having children prior to marriage, to getting married with children. It is a self- reflective chapter, as it allows the reader to examine their potential spouse and themselves, and whether they are ready to commit to marriage. Filled with discussion points, and invaluable tips, this section covers the meat of living life blended.

Inside these pages, you will find the techniques to:
- assure you start your marriage with sound counseling and expectations
- build trust and respect during stepparenting
- learn how to deal with conflict

- how to adjust your life and home when new children are added to your blended family

Part Three - Moving On, Growing Up, Realizing We're All in This Together, After the parents have matured and are at a point where they can cooperate, they can now work together, along with their spouses, to raise their children. In this section, we show you how to develop your family's co-parenting plan, and how to communicate effectively with each other in an attempt to raise a secure child, and sustain a happy marriage.

How to Use This Book

1. Open and Honestly - You will have to look at yourself truthfully while reading this book. If you are in a relationship with someone, be open with each other. If you see your negative traits while reading, don't get upset. Instead, take a look at the information so that you can be a better parent and/or spouse in your blended family. Most importantly, if you have no children yet, look at the responsibilities that may lie ahead of you. Ask yourself if you are ready to make the full commitment of raising a child emotionally and financially; and everything that comes with the possibility of being in a blended family.

2. Multiple Viewpoints - In the chapters, you will find information addressed to a specific group (biological parents, the ex, the spouse, the stepparent). Be sure to read all of the information, whether or not it applies to you, so that you can identify and be aware of what the other people are experiencing. After all, you ALL are raising the same child(ren).

3. Get in Group Discussions - This book stimulates you to discuss this subject not only with your family and loved ones, but also with your children, and other people. When

you have learned some of the techniques discussed in *The Blended Family Survival Guide*, share the information with someone else that is in a similar situation.

4. Keep it as a reference - I can remember when I became a new mother, I looked for every book imaginable that would prepare me for the journey of motherhood! At each change my body experienced, I would refer to my "manual" to understand what was happening, and look ahead to what I should expect for the next phase of change. You will find that *The Blended Family Survival Guide* will become a timeless reference manual, as you use it to navigate through life with your ever-changing blended family or as a single parent.

5. Visit with us online - I have put together an interactive online resource for readers of *The Blended Family Survival Guide* at www.theblendedfamilysurvivalguide.com. There you will find a number of features designed to help you learn and grow in your blended family.

Disclaimer

The information in this book is here to educate and to inform, and we are not liable for your relationships. We highly suggest you seek legal council for matters that require such attention. The legal information in The Blended Family Survival Guide is not designed to be a substitution for sound legal counsel. The identity of individuals depicted in situations throughout this book have been changed to protect their privacy.

Part One

Truth or Consequences

Chapter 1
Choices

Finding Out What's Behind Door #1!

The life we currently live exists because of a series of choices that we made in the past. What the future holds, will in part, be determined by choices and decisions that we make today.

When we were young, the extent of our choices may have been whether to eat oatmeal or frosted flakes, to play in the band or tryout for the football team, or to wear the purple mini-dress or our favorite jeans. As we get older, we are faced with more critical choices that have major consequences.

The effects of our choices may not be seen immediately and may impact our lives only temporarily. Other choices may show their true impact over longer periods of time, consequently affecting multiple areas of our lives indefinitely.

One thing is for certain; everyday,
God gives us twenty-four hours of free will choices.

We feel on top of the world when we are sure we have made the right choice, and full of regret when we haven't chosen poorly. Some choices are fairly easy to make and require just a quick moment of thought, while others may take days, even weeks to deliberate.

If you choose to watch television and hang out instead of preparing a report, the consequence is that you will have to forgo sleep to complete it, be ill-prepared to present it, or even take a chance at completely tanking at the entire assignment.

If you choose to run a marathon, but don't train for it properly, your consequence may be that you pull a muscle, don't finish the race, and are unable to even get out of the bed the next day.

In fact, a series of good choices is what can lead a person to make history in the White House. While just one poor choice, influenced by uncontrolled emotions, can send a person to the jail house.

Our choices will have positive or negative effects on our entire lives as they become fluid chain reactions; even making a seemingly harmless act transform into something catastrophic.

It all boils down to the choices we make.

Because almost everyone can identify with a great dessert, let's take for example something as simple as a doughnut. Choosing to eat one doughnut a couple days out of the week, on the surface may appear harmless. So harmless, that you may find yourself stopping by and grabbing a hot doughnut a couple of times a week on your way into work.

After a few weeks, you notice that your pants are fitting pretty snug in the waist. In fact, you are having problems buttoning them!

This is the time to make a choice to stop eating the doughnuts while you can recover fairly easy, or keep with your morning indulgence that has now become a ritual, or a bad habit.

You make the choice to continue eating doughnuts and find yourself desiring other junk food that you have added to your diet.

Within a year, you have gained several pounds, and are faced with another choice; you can either stop eating the junk and work to get rid of the added pounds, or proceed to continue your bad diet.

Those that choose to keep eating poorly may find themselves overweight and encountering all kinds of health problems (diabetes, high cholesterol, and high blood pressure). The choice to continue eating poorly can lead to being on medications indefinitely, heart attacks, strokes, and even death.

These consequences can become life-altering events, all from the one small choice to eat a doughnut on the way to work.

Then there are the more obvious choices that we make to determine our destiny that I like to call "Life Choices". These choices impact your entire life tremendously and have long-lasting consequences. Life Choices determine whether you are happy or dissatisfied, wealthy or just making ends meet, if you wake up to blue skies and palm trees as opposed to shoveling snow, or if you spend your golden years gazing into your 75-year-old bride's eyes and still see the same glimmer that captivated you at 25.

Some major Life Choices are:
- Going to college
- Starting a career or business
- Where you live
- The people you associate with that influence you
- Who you marry
- How you take care of your health
- Who and what you worship

In between the obvious major Life Choices will be several opportunities to make what appear to be smaller choices. While many people would consider eating that same doughnut mentioned earlier as a "small" choice, we have shown that the doughnuts can become a Life Choice with major negative consequences.

One "small" choice that many people take for granted is who, if, and when they choose to become sexually intimate. This may appear to be a small choice because some people don't look at the act of engaging in sex as a big deal. That is why they will have numerous partners, non-meaningful relationships, and play Russian Roulette with their lives, bodies, and spirits under the auspice that this is a normal part of life.

Normal, until the pregnancy test or STD reads positive.

Contrary to popular belief, when two people engage in a non-marital sexual encounter, whether they realize it or not, they have made a choice. They have to look at the fact that a child could be conceived as a result of sex. When they choose to move forward with their choice, they are choosing to possibly create not only a new life, but a new life path that includes the consequences of their "Life Choice".

Nothing affects life more drastically and suddenly then a child. When you become responsible for the care of a child, you not only have to make good choices for yourself, but now those choices become predicated on how it will affect your child.

This one choice impacts all of your Life Choices, and your entire future.

The Wake Up Call
Let's assume that through a choice, two individuals now have a baby. What does life look like for the two new parents?

How The Man's Life Is Affected By An Unexpected Pregnancy

Fathering Children as a Young Man Turns Boys into Men
Young men who have children early in life interfere with their own coming-of- age and future by taking on the responsibility of being a father at a time when they are still in need of being parented themselves. The young man who becomes a father is thrust into making grown-up decisions and taking adult actions when he should be out playing basketball, video games, and thinking about what he wants to do with his future.

In many cases young fathers try to fit into a role that they are not prepared to assume, nor have any reference for, based on their short lived life experiences. Even worse, many young males do not have the home environment that has given them a living example of what a well-rounded family should be like – their mentors and peers are usually not people who have made a decision to:

- Wait for the right woman
- Wait until they have their lives in order
- Believe that a child is a lifetime commitment

Your Own Success May Have to Be Delayed

When young men become fathers, they are aborting a purpose they could have fulfilled somewhere else; or at the very least, delayed the things they should have been setting out to accomplish at this stage of their lives.

Even with a promising future, the young father may have to choose working at his local fast food joint for diapers and formula, and may have to drop out of school all together. With scholarships, dating, and a social life gone, their money and time will have to be focused on supporting a child.

While it is hard enough to become a success when you have few responsibilities, trying to succeed when you have to take care of a child, earn money to support the child, and deal with the extra demands from the mother who may be trying to do the best she can as well, makes achieving success even more difficult.

Some very responsible men will work harder because they are honorable, while others will settle for their current life status and live off of others – namely their parents.

Not only is the young father's life affected, but his parents' also. It is not unusual for parents to contribute their resources and time to raise their grandchild. Should the young man still be able to attend college or begin a career, the new baby may spend more time with the mom or the father's parents.

When that same young man grows older and wiser, and decides he has found the person he wants to marry, he will bring his child, the baby's mama, and all the baggage he acquired in his early years into his marriage.

Being Someone's Baby's Daddy

When you have children outside of a serious relationship, you run the chance of creating a child with someone that you would not normally choose to be the mother of your child. The woman, who may have seemed so hot a couple of days ago, may turn into your worst nightmare should she become the mother of your child.

For some men, the pregnancy is the result of a completely sexual relationship, while the woman may have considered herself to be in a serious relationship. Nevertheless, when you start having relationships outside of marriage and a child is born, you will become responsible for the child and will have to relate to your child through the mother.

The man will be expected to take on the role of a father and some fathers even take on what they consider the role of a husband. Unfortunately, out of fear, some men will run away from the new responsibility earning the title of the "deadbeat dad", others will perform in the role half-heartedly being the " baby's daddy", while others will make attempts to make it work; the best way they know how.

The Possibility Of Another Man Raising Your Child

If you're not going to be involved in the child's life, or if you do not live with your child, it is very likely that some other man may eventually play a part of raising your son or daughter. Should the mother decide to get married and has custody of the child, your child will have another man parenting them on a daily basis. The father will have to be prepared for the emotions he may experience with the reality that there may be another father figure in his child's life, and work to not act foolishly should another man come in his child's life.

If You Decide To Marry Someone Else

If and when the man decides to get married and has had children from previous relationships, he will not be able to have his first child with his wife because he has already had that experience (maybe a couple of times before settling down). While marriage itself is challenging, the man will come to his marriage with baggage from past relationships and will have to communicate with ex-girlfriends, because of the child.

Naming Jr.

If the man named his first child after himself, he can never have that honor bestowed on the child he has with his wife; though younger men probably don't take that into consideration because they are thinking only about their current life circumstance. This is yet another decision that the man who has had children before marriage has made, which will affect his future wife, his current child(ren), and any future children he decides to have with his wife. All as a result of a choice he made years before his marriage.

The father will have to make sure he has a strong marriage, including a strong woman who's able to accept him, his children, and everything that goes along with parenting children outside of a marriage.

A Lifetime of Commitment From a One-Night Stand

In the words of Kanye West from the song Gold Digger, "18 years, 18 years, she's got one of your kids, got you for 18 years". The sentiment of this verse rings true for so many men around the world. Once you have a child with someone, in the court's eyes you are financially obligated to them for 18 years. Although you may feel trapped until your child comes of age, the real victim is the child, as they come here innocent and not a participant of what led to them arriving on this planet.

Regardless, if you are in a committed relationship, married, or unmarried, when you have a child with someone, for the next 18 years, whether you like it or not, you will have to deal, relate, and communicate with the mother of your child. At social gatherings, school events, and in everyday life, no matter if the relationship is pleasant or from the pit of hell. You got them, or should I say they might have you, for at least

18 years! So, make your decisions wisely and be responsible with the choices you make.

How The Woman's Life Is Affected By An Unexpected Pregnancy

Along with many of the same things that the man experiences, as mentioned earlier, the woman will have to contend with some additional elements.

Responsibility Starts From Day 1

Not only do women bear the responsibility of being a mother, but they also have to physically carry the child - so they take on a whole different prospective from men.

For the woman, responsibility starts the moment they find out that they have a new life growing inside of them. At that moment they become a mother, and the life of that child depends on how they care for their baby - even in the womb. Their parental role starts immediately, as they begin to provide nourishment for the child developing inside of them, adapt to the changes of their body and mind, and conform their life and schedule. All of this happens even before the child is born!

Whereas, the man may feel the reality of the child only when the woman begins showing or when the child is actually born, the woman is immediately thrust into parenthood, and becomes the vessel used to birth a new life.

Having His Child Doesn't Guarantee He Will Stay

You love him and want to spend the rest of your life with him. Oh, how cute! The baby will have his eyes, and your nose. Get a grip! Come back to reality, and think about what you're signing up for lady!

Ask women around the world if they want to be swept off their feet or if they dream of the day they will find Mr. Right, and they will say "yes". Unfortunately for some women Mr. Right Now is what they end up settling for, even when they desire a serious relationship, and marriage.

During the course of the pregnancy and especially after giving birth, the mother may desire to settle into having a family with the father of her child – fully immersing into family life. In fact, a woman could move from being single, to pregnant, to living with someone in a blink of an eye.

Should the woman start living with the father of her soon to be child, it can create a false reality to them both as they assume the roles of husband and wife with zero commitment. Unfortunately, statistics show that the rates are low for people who cohabitate to actually marry each other. If the woman is not married to the father, they also stand the chance of having neither financial nor emotional support from the father of their child. It's a fact that, more than half of unwed mothers end up raising their child as a single parent, with all of the responsibilities falling entirely on them.

You May Be the Major Influence in His/Her Life
If the father is not around on a consistent basis, the woman will serve as both mother and father to their child. There will be little downtime to follow their own dreams and life path. They won't get the opportunity to say, "Go ask your Dad", if the father is not around. Instead, they will always have to provide solutions, serving the role of both mommy and daddy.

You May, or Will Be the Main Provider
If the mother becomes the main provider due to lack of child support and other resources from the father, she will have to be prepared to provide all the necessities for their child (ren). She may have to pick up extra hours at work, delay her dreams, and change educational plans, to establish long-term financial security for her family.

You Will Need a Support Group

In the absence of the father, the mother will need a support group which she can rely on, that should consist of her immediate family, friends, and adult male figures. When she has to be at work, or away from the child, she will have to develop a team of people that she can trust to meet the needs of her child.

Emotional Battles

Feelings of resentment, unforgiveness, abandonment, and loneliness are going to be natural when the woman is a single mom. The reality that she will have to heal and rid herself of these negative feelings before she can move on to a fulfilling relationship and positively raise her children is necessary.

Physical Adjustment

The mother will have to adjust to everything that comes with having a child: stretch marks, mood swings and weight gain. To top all of the normal feelings associated with pregnancy, imagine having to feel insecure and questioning if the man you're having a child with will want be around. These insecurities are what make women want to jump from the delivery table to the treadmill to stay attractive to the father.

Happily Ever, Never

The creation of a child is such a unifying process between a woman and man that it makes us realize why it was intended for the institution of marriage. The powerful and meaningful event of creating another human being with your DNA, seeing it grow inside the mother, yet still having no commitment between the two people who created the life, is troubling. It explains why women feel alone and upset when they have to experience this miracle and face the future alone. The reality of 'it's just you and baby' lives in the shattered hopes of becoming a family.

You Are a Package Deal

When non-custodial fathers date, or marry, they still are seen as an individual. This is not so with a woman whose child lives with them. If you are not in a relationship with the father of your child and begin to date, or marry, you and your child will always be a package deal. The person that the single mom decides to have a relationship with will have to accept that she brings with her a ready-made family. They will have a full- time relationship with not only the single mom but her child as well. If she does marry, she will have to accept the fact that she no longer will be raising her child alone, and will have to allow her spouse to discipline her child. The mother will have to relinquish all of the 'I'm doing this by myself attitude', allowing her new spouse to participate in the parenting of her child.

Living unselfishly

The instinctive nature of a mother is to nourish her child, consider her child's needs first, and provide an atmosphere for her child to succeed. If the mother is a little selfish, having a baby will change her self-centered attitude quickly; whether she's ready to accept the challenge or not.

A Note To Men And Women

The Four Areas of Responsibility
Both Parents Must Provide

The Emotional / Mental Responsibility

The emotional security of children plays a significant role in shaping their lives - from their *personality, confidence, success in future relationships, and mental health* -- as they grow. It is a widely accepted fact that children from loving, caring households go on to become well-adjusted adults, while children from abusive, broken, or neglectful homes often grow up to have serious emotional or even mental problems.

In Dr. Biringen's book, *Raising a Secure Child: Creating an Emotional Connection Between You and Your Child*, she writes that when children are emotionally secure, some of the benefits are: Children are less likely to show forms of insecure patterns of attachment in parent-child relationships.

- Children from emotionally available homes have *better peer relationships.*

- Children who have emotionally available relationships with their parents are *less aggressive* and less likely to be the targets of aggression from other children. They are also more socially skilled and more accepted by their peers.

- Children who have emotionally available relationships with their parents are more *attentive in school.*

- Children from emotionally available homes seem to *relate better with their teachers,* engaging in less conflict with them.

The Physical Responsibility

The physical responsibility includes making sure the child is nourished, physically healthy, and provided with the financial assistance for medical insurance. The physical responsibility also includes making sure the child is in a safe environment.

The Financial Responsibility

As a parent, it is your responsibility to financially support your child until they reach 18 years of age. For many, the financial responsibility of supporting their children will extend beyond the age of 18 if the child is attending college.

When a child's parents are unmarried or divorced, child support is awarded to the parent who has custody (with whom the child is living).

The Moral, Spiritual, and Social Responsibility

As a parent, it is your responsibility to teach your child about morals and make them spiritually aware. Children are wired to look to their parents for guidance, and it is the parents' job to lead them into being a productive member of society. Children naturally want to please their parents, be loved, understood, and seek the approval of their parents. Because of this admiration, children will often imitate their parents, so parents have to be sure they are good role models!

- Being honest and operating with integrity sends a message to your child about trust.

- When you are generous, it teaches them about giving, sharing, and caring for others. Their kindness will come from you being gentle. Your children will reciprocate your respect for others in conversations and at home as they imitate your respectful behavior.

- Having a positive outlook, attitude, and encouraging words, gives them hope. Your child's spirituality and their relationship with God originates from you and how you relate to God.

- They watch not what you say, but what you do, both at home and in your place of worship.

When children live in two separate homes, establishing their moral and spiritual values can be difficult if both parents do not share the same views. For example, if the custodial parent puts little focus on providing sound moral and spiritual values, and the non-custodial parent has strong values and spiritual awareness, the non-custodial parent will have a limited time to instill their values and pass on their beliefs. Should that happen, the place where the child spends the majority of their time may be the major influence, good or bad.

What a Strong Father Figure in a Child's Life Provides:

- Provides stability

- Helps build self-esteem

- Acknowledges identity and self-worth for girls

- Builds confidence and strength in boys

- Shows children they are loved

- Children who have strong father figures are less likely to get involved in gangs and criminal behavior.

- Children who have good relationships with their fathers usually grow up to have good relationships with their own children.

- Fathers instill generational history, and pass down the traditions of their family to their children so they feel welcomed and loved.

- If the father is active, his presence helps the children to lead an active life.

- A father treating his wife well shows children a role model of a healthy relationship, and teaches them about relating to others.

- A healthy father-child relationship discourages the need to use drugs and/or alcohol for fulfillment.

- Children with active fathers in their lives are more likely to graduate from school.

Two More Important Points To Remember Should A Child Be Conceived:

#1 Communication Will Be the Key in Raising a Stable Child
It does not matter what happened between the two of you, who was right or wrong. What matters now is that both of you, as

parents, keep the lines of communication open in regards to the child(ren).

#2 The Two of You Will Forever Be in Each Other's Life

In one way or another, for at least 18 years, you will be a part of each other's life. School activities, proms, social gatherings, and decision making, may all include your ex. The sooner you come to grips with that, the better.

Many people have grown up in single parent homes having only sub-par relationships with their fathers. Having an unexpected child does not mean that life is over or that you cannot have a healthy child and a successful, happy life. What it does mean however, is that you will be faced with a journey of challenges, healing, endurance, and most of all, selflessness.

Ask any single parent and they will tell you that it is difficult raising a child alone and that they wished they had someone to share in the experience and responsibilities on a daily basis.

If you are reading this book and have not yet had a child, remember that your choices impact the rest of your life. Deciding to have a child is not a "small" decision, it is a Life Choice. It will affect all aspects of your life. It is not by any means something that should be anything less than well thought out, and done with someone who will be there for the long haul.

Choose Wisely

Chapter 2
Understanding Child Custody

A Child Is Born, But Where Do They Live?

Custody:
A guarding or keeping safe; providing care and protection.

When a child has two biological parents who live with each other, both parents are responsible for making choices together (where the child will live, whether he goes to public or private school, if he can go to a sleepover at his classmates house, or even what church to attend). The parents work synergistically to make the best decisions possible for their child.

However, if the parents are no longer together or divorce, there will be two very important questions that the parents will have to determine:

- Who will primarily be responsible for making choices about the child's life?

- Where will the child live?

Undeniably, whether together or separated, both parents have values and knowledge that are equally important to contribute to their children's lives. Therefore, both parent's presence in the child's life is monumental. This is why it is so important that parents endeavor to workout a plan where their child will still receive the

16

things each of them innately have to offer, despite the fact that they no longer choose, or may have never chosen to be together.

In any separation situation, custody can encompass many things other than the physical place where the child resides. In fact, in some cases, it can become more about control, power, and money.

Regardless of the circumstance, the establishment of where the child lives should be based on this primary idea - who will have the ability to raise the child the best?

When negative feelings and experiences have transpired between the parents, they may find themselves having a difficult time separating their personal feelings that influence the way they feel about the other parent's parental abilities. Those negative feelings may influence whether the parent can have visitation, how often they see the child, and how they provide for the child.

In some cases, one of the parents might walk away completely from their parental responsibilities, leaving the remaining parent to raise the child alone. Men site various reasons for walking away, from questioning whether the child is their own, to getting frustrated with enduring the mother's drama in an effort to have a relationship with the child. Another matter to recognize is that many men, and women, lack basic parenting skills, which causes the courts to limit the amount of influence a parent can have on the child through the restriction of physical contact.

Except for in extreme cases, if the two parents were not married, the child automatically will be in the mother's custody from birth, with the father having visitation rights. Although the father might believe that he has a natural "right" to see his child, additional measures may have to be taken legally to assure specific allocated visitation if the two parents can't come to an agreement and cordially interact as adults. In this case, the father would have to petition the court for additional legal rights, establish a visitation order, or even file a motion for custody, which could become a custody battle. This is where it can get really ugly. If one parent wants nothing to do with the other, custody battles are sometimes launched with the intent that if one parent is awarded sole custody, the other parent basically disappears, or has very little say in the upbringing of the child. The parents go to court in a win/lose frame of mind. Winning is expected to mean that one parent gets what they want, and what many battling parents want is to eliminate the other parent from theirs and the children's life.

On the other hand, many parents find themselves in court when the parent is negating their responsibilities, as in not seeing their child, or lack of providing child support.

When discussing custody, there are critical pieces of information that you need to know before making the decision of whom the child will stay with, and who will ultimately make the life decisions regarding the child. Below are some definitions you should know, as well as the criteria that the courts consider when determining who will get custody.

Custodial Parent

The Custodial Parent is the term that is used for the parent that has primary physical custody of a child. Typically the child resides with the custodial parent.

Non-Custodial Parent

The term Non-Custodial parent is a term used for the parent that has the child for a lesser amount of time. The child only visits or resides with the non-custodial parent during the time that the Non-Custodial Parent exercises his/her visitation right with the child in a separate residence.

Physical custody

Physical custody is the right of a parent to have the child live with them. A parent can have sole physical custody but share legal custody. This means that although the child primarily lives with one parent, the other parent has a say in making the major decisions for the child's welfare, education, and life, if they so desire.

Legal Custody

Legal Custody refers to the absolute decision-making authority for a minor child. This can be awarded to both parents if the judge sees them as morally and financially responsible people.

Why Determining Legal Custody Becomes Important

What happens when one of the parents feels that their daughter should be able to get the third piercing in their ear? When should the daughter start dating? What do they do when the son is hanging around the wrong crowd and a decision to restrict him from seeing specific individuals is necessary?

These are some of the many questions that parents have a hard time agreeing on when both parents' views are different. Often the custodial parent will make the majority of the decisions because they are closer to the situation and spend more time with the child. The other side of this picture is that in many cases, both parents want to have equal say in the welfare of the child because they have ethical differences of opinion.

This is when it is critical to establish each parent's legal custody status along with the custody and visitation order. If one parent has sole legal custody, it means that the other parent literally has no legal say in what happens in the child's life.

Sole Custody

Sole Custody is when the parent has been awarded full legal and physical custody. The parent who doesn't have sole custody usually has visitation with the right only to spend time with the child, but without any decision-making authority.

Sole Legal Custody

Sole Legal Custody is when the parent has been awarded full legal and physical custody. The parent who doesn't have sole custody may or may not have visitation with the child, without decision-making authority.

Sole Physical Custody

Sole Physical Custody is when the child remains with one parent on a full time basis, and the other parent is excluded from having any physical custody of the child. Typically this is when a parent has abused or neglected the child.

Joint Legal Custody

Joint Legal Custody is when both parents participate in reaching decisions regarding the health, education and welfare of the child.

Joint or Shared Custody

Joint or Shared custody refers to an arrangement in which both the care and authority are shared by both parents.

Joint or shared custody occurs when the children alternate between both parents' homes within a normal week. Joint custody orders can change when the children become teenagers, as they are likely to prefer a single residence as opposed to splitting the time equally. This decision evolves mainly due to the child's increased school or social activities and their desire to be in one place were most of their friends live.

About Joint Custody Issues

While joint custody may be good for maintaining contact with both parents, it can create additional problems. Constantly transporting the children between two houses can create anxiety and insecurity in children when they feel they don't actually have one permanent home. Parents should ask themselves if the needs of their child is the motivating factor behind the decision of joint custody and not their own desires, their need to get back at the other parent, or as a way of getting out of paying child support.

School and Joint Physical Custody

While the children are attending school, joint custody schedules can be a challenge, especially as the children become more active in school-related events. The most effective way this can work for parents who share custody, is for the parents to live close to each other so the child can attend the same school with the same friends. If this does not happen and there are problems with getting the child to school on time or problems because one parent lives in a different school district, this can inevitably make a child feel like an outsider.

The more consistent the child's life is,
the more adjusted the child will be.

Another suggestion for school-aged children could be for one parent to have custody during the week, and the other on weekends, especially when there is considerable distance between the two households. The parent who doesn't see the child during the week may be able to have more visitations during the summer, holidays, and school breaks. The only negative to this particular arrangement is that the parent who has the child during the week will never be able to plan activities for the child on the weekend, unless a separate arrangement is set up with the other parent.

The most important thing is for the two parents to really talk to each other and come to an arrangement that will most benefit the child. Parents having this discussion need to lower their defenses and approach the issue from the standpoint of what's most convenient for the children. The determining factor should be how the schedule will allow the child to have the best quality and meaningful time with each parent, while creating or maintaining a stable environment that allows the child to establish friendships with their peers.

When Joint Custody Is Used as a Way of Getting Out of Paying Child Support

When both parents equally share custody of the child, no one receives or pays child support. Often this is a tactic used by one of the parents to avoid paying child support. When done with the wrong motive, the deceptive parent may drop off the child at relative's homes, and never actually spend time with the child. In reality, the parent either may not have the time in their daily schedules, or won't make the time for the child. This parent's goal is to be able to find a way around paying the support while still having joint say in the child's life.

Reasons For Change In Custody

When the Non-Custodial Parent Is Denied Visitation

It is not uncommon to see situations where the non-custodial parent may feel that the custodial parent is making it extremely difficult to see their child, or purposely keeping the child away from them, even though there is a visitation order in place. The non-custodial parent may get fed up and feel the only way they will have relationship with their child is by gaining joint or even legal custody.

Filing for a change in custody is an occurrence that happens often between parents when the custodial parent may want nothing to do with the other parent, and denies visitation as a form of control. The custodial parent would do much better gritting their teeth and obeying the rules despite their personal feelings, in order to avoid ending up in court. Usually, a move from the non-custodial parent seeking custody is a desperate action taken by a denied parent in hopes of having a relationship with their child.

The Custodial Parent Wants to Move Out of State

When it comes to child custody, relocation is a hot-button issue. Some custodial parents may want to relocate with their children in order to pursue a job change, be closer to family members, or to get a fresh start. However, the decision to move out of state should not be taken lightly.

First, the child custody laws in your state must be considered. Each state has different relocation laws, and some states do require written consent from the non-custodial parent. Therefore, you'll want to know of any particular statutes in your state that could affect your decision. Seeking the counsel of a qualified family law attorney will also help you understand the implications of a custodial parent's decision to move out of state.

Second, if your ex does contest your request to move out of state with the children, you should also be prepared for a full custody evaluation. In particular, be prepared to show:

- How the move will result in a better quality-of- life for your child(ren). If this is a job, is it more money to aid in providing for the child? Does it have better health insurance, etc.

- The extent to which your ex currently exercises their right to spend time with the children.

- That you are willing to allow for longer, less frequent visits if your request to move out of state is approved.

- That you will actively support such changes in the visitation schedule.

- That you are prepared to absorb the increased cost of transportation, or that you and your ex have an agreement on who is paying for the child's travel.

- That the move is not an attempt to restrict the non-custodial parent from access to the child.

Finally, consider carefully the impact this move out of state will have on your children. It is entirely possible that the benefits of increased pay, or closer proximity to extended family members, do not outweigh the benefits your children enjoy right now as a result of a consistent, ongoing, in-person relationship with their other parent.

It is impossible to reduce that relationship to increased phone calls and longer summertime visits without consequences which are sure to appear in your child(ren)'s behavior and attitudes over time. Therefore, it is important to talk openly with your children, and with your ex, about any decision to move out of state. This will ensure that no part of the move is executed in haste.

The Son May Need to Live With His Father, and the Daughter Needs Her Mom

Some parents make decisions early on in their child's life that they will agree to a change in the primary custody when the child becomes a teenager and may need more attention from the non-custodial parent, as in the case with boys becoming men. Even when there are male figures in the young man's life while only living with his mom, there are some invaluable things that can only be delivered from the father. While other males can certainly be surrogates, one cannot negate the fact that young men need their fathers. Even with the exceptional jobs that many single moms do to raise their male children, the son may start acting out in school or show other signs that suggest that the father may need to step in and provide full-time parenting. The same can be said for a teenage lady, although in most cases the switch in custody is more common amongst male children.

Change In the Home Environment of One of the Parents

Change in custody can sometimes become necessary when there are drastic changes in the custodial parent's home environment that has been observed by the non-custodial parent. The financial situation of the custodial parent may have changed, the neighborhood they live in may become dangerous, or the custodial parent may have other excruciating circumstances occurring in their lives that are not in the best interest of their child. These situations may signal a need to change the custody when it results in a better living situation for the child.

Custody Battles

If the parents decide to go their separate ways and agree on custody issues, life is good. They are no legal problems and the courts will not have to be overly involved with the way the parents raise and support their children.

If an agreement can't be reached between the parents, then there is no choice but to work it out in court. A legal dispute can be expensive and emotionally draining for both parents, and children.

What the Courts Consider When Determining Custody

Custody decisions made by the courts are said to be made with the best interests of the child in mind. Judges will differ as to their criteria and definition of what they deem as "best interest". This definition varies from state to state and from jurisdiction to jurisdiction, with their criteria continually changing.

Here are standard factors that judges seem to use in deciding children's custodial issues.

(Please Note: This is not an official statement, and while these are the standard factors from state to state, consult your state's court system and/or an attorney when preparing for a case.)

Moms Sometimes Rule

It's not etched in stone that if you are female you automatically get the children in all states and all courts. However, in general, courts still prefer mothers to fathers when it comes to child custody. In order for the father to have custody, most judges require that the father prove that the mother is unfit or that living conditions are unacceptable.

Some examples of distress are:

- being careless with the children

- abandonment

- offering drugs to the children

- the mother having men around the children who

- could put them in danger or harm

In fact, in an unfortunate turn, today there are more men than in previous years that are gaining custody of their children, because women are favoring relationships with men, careers, and their own freedom over being mothers.

Who Has Consistently Performed Key Parenting Activities for the Child?

Which parent performs the daily, necessary tasks such as laying out the clothes at night, waking them up, brushing teeth, and getting the child to school? Who picks them up from school, fixes the afternoon snack, prepares dinner, and makes sure the homework is correct and complete? Who supervises bath time at night, reads their favorite story, and makes sure that prayers are said?

You get the picture; who actually <u>cares</u> for the child.

Preference for the Status Quo

Most judges want to leave things alone, in other words, if it ain't broke, don't fix it!

For example, if the parents have been separated for several months and the child has been living without any evident problems with the mother, the preference for the father to gain full custody is slim. At the same time, if the child has been alternating between their mother's and father's houses (as in joint custody), most judges would be inclined to allow the court order to remain unless there are circumstances that would warrant a custody change.

Morality

If the parents were married, the parent who has been unfaithful, (particularly if with a succession of different lovers), starts off in the red when it comes to custody. The same goes with a parent who is guilty of breaking the law.

Who Will Help Ensure That the Other Parent Spends Time with the Child?

If one of the parents has consistently interfered or denied visitation, or has made it difficult for the non-custodial parent to see their child, some judges would consider having the child live with the other parent, with the intention that the parent denied visitation will do a better job of allowing parenting time for both parties.

Stability

If the mother seems to have a stable consistent lifestyle which she has not varied from in years, while the father has moved every six months, depending on which girlfriend he's living with, the Mom will definitely benefit from the father's lack of stability. Judges usually believe that the more stable environment will be the most nurturing for children.

Standard of Living

The child's living conditions are another factor that judges will consider when deciding custody. If the mom is living with her cousin, her other two children, and her cousin's three children, all in a one bedroom apartment, and the dad can offer the child its own room, with access to a good school system; the dad will have the inside track.

Track Record of Success

If the child was doing well in school (passing or even average) with one parent, but after moving with the other parent starts receiving bad grades and showing disciplinary problems; courts will consider whether they should be returned to the previous home environment. The same goes for attendance, and to a lesser extent, performance in extracurricular activities.

Quality of School System

Judges pay attention to things like class size, availability of extracurricular activities (particularly of those the child would enjoy), a school's reputation and ranking, and the percentage of the student body that enters college. This can work to the disadvantage of the parent who lives in a lower income area. In the end, it is what's in the child's best interest including educational quality.

Relations with Extended Family

The widely-used saying "It takes a village to raise a child", rings true when referring to custody matters; a village of aunts, uncles, and grandparents. Judges make their decisions about parental custody, and pay attention to the circle of support and opportunities for familial interaction.

The Child's Preference

Below age seven, most judges don't consider the child's preferences. If the parent seems to influence or suggest that the child state their preference, judges do not take kindly to their manipulation of the child. At age 14 or above, judges give more respect and consideration to the preferences of an older child (in some states, the age is 12). Younger children are accommodated based on their maturity level.

If the child younger than 14 with a reasonable explanation for their decision petitions the court, the judge would be more likely to grant the request over that of a nine year old who says " I want to live with my Dad because I have more video games and fun over there".

It also is not unusual for a judge to order a psychological evaluation and a home evaluation before passing judgment.

The Report and Recommendation of Any Expert Witnesses or Other Independent Investigator

Recommendations from therapists, school counselors, teachers, and other credible witnesses are considered in custody cases. Usually the experts have related with the child or parent enough to give a fair recommendation based upon their observation, or other pertinent information.

Other Considerations:

- Confirmed evidence of abuse or neglect

- How either continuing or disrupting the current custody arrangement will affect the children

- The mental and physical health of the parents and the children

- The age of the children

- The wishes of the parents

- The quality of the relationship between the children and each parent

What Happens If the Non-Custodial Parent Makes a Habit of Not Returning the Child at the Correct Time, and You Fear that the Parent Might Not Return with Your Child?

In most states, it's a crime to take a child from his or her parent with the intent to interfere with that parent's physical custody of the child at assigned times (even if the taker also has custody rights). This crime is commonly referred to as "custodial interference." In most states, the parent deprived of custody may sue the taker for damages, as well as get help from the police to have the child returned. Repeat offenders can be denied custodial and/or visitation rights by a judge.

Who Gets Custody When Only One Parent's Name is on the Birth Certificate?

The law differs from state to state. In some states, like Oklahoma, when no father is listed on the birth certificate, it is presumed that the mother has sole custody in cases where the parents were unmarried at the time of the child's birth. You should be aware that many states either make no presumption of custody based on the birth certificate, or presume joint custody even in cases where the parents were never married.

Therefore, take the time to familiarize yourself with the domestic relations statutes in the state where you live. It is possible that you will need to formally file for custody, even though your child is already living with you.

Custody Can Always Be Renegotiated

No custody (or visitation) arrangement is final. Decisions made (whether between individuals or by the courts) can be changed or renegotiated when circumstances change by filing paperwork and meeting before a judge.

Chapter 3
The Weekend Lover

The Art of Visitation Revealed

Visitation and Parenting Time

When a young man sees his father care for his wife and provide for his family, he learns about respect and responsibility. Likewise, when a young girl sees a woman taking care of her home, while still balancing work, the young woman is taught how to be both a nurturer and a businesswoman, or as I like to say, "make the bacon and cook it!" Even if we are not intentionally setting out to teach our children, we are shaping our children's value system everyday.

In a two-parent home, children have the daily opportunity to relate to both their mother and father, as well as learn how to work together as a family unit. When the parents do not live together, the non-custodial parent will have to make sure they still play an active role in the growth of their child, using their time wisely to impact their children's life as they would if they were with them everyday.

Enter the Visitation Order

A Visitation Order is an order that establishes consistent scheduled time for the non-custodial parent to spend with their child (ren) and is also known as a "parenting-time" order.

In a perfectly blended world, separated or divorced parents would be able to talk with each other to decide how to split or share their parenting time. They would decide the specific days and times that the non-custodial parent would see their child. In this ideal situation, the courts stay out of the picture, and decisions about the children would be worked out by the parents.

Although it would be great if both the parents could work together, unfortunately, that is not the norm. In cases where the parents tend to disagree and argue, it would be much simpler to have an official order filed with the family court to give less opportunity for conflict where decisions cannot be reached amicably.

Some Models of Visitation Time

Model #1 - Every Other Weekend
(Friday 6:00 p.m. to Sunday 6:00 p.m.)

This parenting plan option establishes twelve days separation from the non-custodial parent. It severely limits opportunities for involvement in the child's day-to-day, school, homework, and extra-curricular activities. When parents have visitation every other weekend, they usually ask for half of the summer vacation and alternating holidays.

Model #2 - Every Other Weekend Plus Midweek Visit
(Friday 6:00 p.m. to Sunday 6:00 p.m., and every Wednesday 5:00 p.m. to 8:00 p.m.)
This parenting plan option limits separation from the second parent to seven days. However, adding the midweek transition could allow for more conflict on the transition back to the first parent's home. Some non-custodial parents describe the evening-only visit as too rushed with less time to complete homework and "settle in".

Model #3 - Every Other Weekend Plus Midweek Overnight
(Friday 6:00 p.m. to Sunday 6:00 p.m., and Wednesday 5:00 p.m. to Thursday 8:00 a.m.)

This parenting plan option limits separation from the second parent to six days. It also allows greater opportunity for the non-custodial parent to supervise homework and to participate in bedtime and waking rituals. This option allows for transition at school after the midweek overnight; avoiding parental contact and potential conflict. The midweek overnight also affords the custodial parent a regularly scheduled break in caretaking responsibilities.

Quality Parenting Time During Visitation

*Things the non-custodial parent can do to make
the most out of visiting time with their child
by preparing for their child's visit*

Plan Activities

Take the time out to plan special activities for you and your child on their weekend visit. This time is very special to your child, and although it may feel routine to the parent, most children really look forward to their special weekend visit. So plan for success! From roller-skating to movies, or maybe even a day in the park, create memorable moments for you and your child to enjoy. Even if you don't have the budget for a grand adventure, you would be surprised how much fun you can have when you put some effort into making the magic happen!

At the end of each visit, question your child to see what else they may be interested in doing on their next visit. This is the time when you can create your own family rituals that your child can look forward to over the years.

Go Grocery Shopping

If you are used to feasting on microwave dinners and takeout, consider shopping for snack food, cook breakfast or dinner, and include some of their favorite treats too! This will create a comfortable routine while saving a few dollars.

Clean Your House & Prepare a Special Area or Room

Make sure your home is in guest mode by making it spick-and-span as you would if your favorite relative were coming to town! Prepare an area or room for your child that they can call their own. If it's a room, add special touches like pictures of the two of you, or their favorite poster; something that connects them to the space.

Alter Your Social Life

If you are single, let your friends know it's your child's weekend so they won't drop by unexpectedly, leave crazy voicemails that your child may hear, or behave inappropriately around your child. Regardless to your personal life you live aside from your child, honor your parental role and adjust your lifestyle. Put your best parent foot forward!

Arrive On Time

Arriving on schedule to pick up your child for your visitation time demonstrates predictability and creates stability. Make sure to bring your child back on time too! Should a change occur in your schedule, inform the other parent, and confirm they're OK with the change. Always try to be considerate of the other parent's time.

Keep a Positive Attitude

Picking up and bringing your children back to their parent may sometimes be an uncomfortable experience. Your ex may always seem to have a few words to say to you, or may use the drop-off time to discuss matters that would be best discussed at a more appropriate time. Strive to be polite, but defer to discuss issues later when children are not present. Your buttons may really get pushed, but do not let anyone take away from the relationship that you are maintaining with your children. They would be negatively influenced if you got into an argument. The positive benefit is that when your children see you being polite, they will remember it and witness firsthand how to resolve conflict with integrity.

Be True to Your Word. Keep Your Visitation Time Regular and Consistent

One of the goals of a visitation order is that it creates a set schedule for the non-custodial parent to share consistent time with their children. If it's your time to visit, don't let other things in your life interfere. There is nothing sadder than the image of a child sitting with a suitcase, staring out the window for a parent who doesn't show. Keep your visits, even if it means you have to reschedule other things. Make that time with your child your number one priority.

I can remember a few Fridays when I ran anxiously to the door hoping it was my father each time I heard a car come down our street. As the day became night, my mother would try to make up for the fact that my father did not come to pick me up. My mother would have to quickly, and creatively think of ways to take my attention off the disappointment, and shift towards something positive. She alone had to answer all of my questions as to "why" my father wasn't coming.

For years, I would have to get over the fear of feeling that things I really desired weren't going to happen; a result of the uncertainty created from memories of my visitation with my father. This became an issue that I had to conquer as an adult, and one that I am sure my father had no idea of the consequences I would suffer by his choices.

If you are the custodial parent, make sure the child is available on the non-custodial parent's weekend, and don't withhold visitation when angry over other issues. When a child is not allowed to see both parents, they suffer the greatest loss.

Don't Let Distance Interfere With Visitation

If the non-custodial parent is living some distance away, make definite arrangements for when and how the child will visit the other parent. In these cases, longer visits may be in order, such as spring break, holiday weekends, or summer vacation.

Don't Let Guilt Make You Become a "Buddy" to Your Child Instead of a Parent

A problem with some non-custodial parents is their inability to discipline their children, especially on their visitation weekend. This is usually found to occur when the non-custodial parent has been at the mercy of the custodial parent as to when they can see their child. The parent may feel that when they finally see their child, they don't want to spend the time chastising them; they just want to enjoy the visit. The parent can feel so insecure about seeing their child regularly and not wanting to "rock the boat", so to speak, that they don't want to do anything that would discourage the child's visit. To a degree, it is completely understandable. They must also remember that this is their opportunity to parent their child, transfer knowledge, and reinforce behavioral expectations.

If you are trying to correct behavior and your time has been limited with your child, use your own judgment for the extent of discipline. It may be that you will have to enforce the correction of the behavior over a few visits instead of entirely during the occurrence.

In the end, you must feel comfortable with the way you parent your child. Do not be afraid that if you discipline them, they won't want to see you. A lot of character formation can be instilled during leisure as well as difficult times. Don't feel like you are ruining your time with your child because you have to discipline them when necessary. If it all works for the betterment of the child and the respect level in your relationship, then it needs to be done.

Talking to Your Children

Having a court order that dictates when you are allowed to physically interact with your child will spill over to verbal communication as well. Parents tend to unconsciously limit their communication with their child to their time of visitation. Another deterrent is when the non-custodial parent may not want to call to speak to the child because it means they have to speak or interact with a difficult ex.

One of the many goals of The Blended Family Survival Guide is to increase communication, maturity, respect, and responsibility amongst parents, so that they can raise healthy, secure children separately, yet together. If one of the parents is trying to communicate with their child, every effort should be made to make the connection happen, despite your personal feelings about the parent.

The Internet has also become a great tool to stay in touch with your family. You can send your children emails and special cards, as well as aid them with their homework through Internet tools like Skype and texting.

Staying in contact with your child, even when you don't see them, will help to assure that although you are not together, you're always thinking about them.

Give Your Child a Visitation Calendar
Purchase a pocket calendar or create a calendar page and highlight the days your children will spend with you. This way, your children will know when they will see you next; and it will give them something to look forward to. If children have cell phones with calendars or Ipods, you can load your visitation days.

Structure, Cohesiveness, and Consistency are Keys
Set rules for your house. Have your child abide by those rules, and create definite structure in your household. This will give the child stability, as he or she will know that "this is the routine at my Mom's house and this is the routine at my Dad's house". Ideally, one of the best solutions to create structure in the child's life would be for the parents to discuss how they could best establish similar home environments to benefit the child. (To see examples of this, read Chapter 14 on Cooperative Parenting.)

If the Custodial Parent Is Single, and the Non-Custodial Parent is Married, It Provides a Balanced Life View Through Seeing a Married Couple Interact

Parents in a healthy marriage, greatly benefit the child by providing a point of reference and a sense of permanency in a child's life.

When children see only live-in boyfriends and girlfriends, they will have an incomplete exposure to the positive impact of solid partnership. But when a child can see a wife and husband in a committed, stable environment, it establishes them as a family unit in the child's eyes.

Although there are many single mothers raising great men and women, statistics show that children who grow up in loving, married households are more likely to seek that same kind of stable relationship in marriage.

The parent who is newly married has to be aware that their child may feel their time is being invaded with the addition of someone new, especially if the child was used to having the parent to themselves.

It is imperative that the married parent spends joint time with their child and spouse as well as one-on-one time with just the child. The shared time will knit the new relationship into a family one, and the personal time with the non-custodial parent provides for bonding and security.

When Visitation Goes Wrong

Deprogramming

Deprogramming is a term used to mean the process of "unlearning" observed negative behaviors and actions.

When the two households are considerably different, either of the parents, may feel like they need to deprogram the child's attitude and behavior after spending time with the other parent.

Example 1
The mother is the custodial parent, and the home environment is filled with a lot of profanity, negative talking, and depression.

The child can visit the father's house, and by contrast, the father's home may live in an environment where there is a positive outlook, deep spirituality, and affirmation. The father will then have to pour concentrated efforts into impacting his child in a short period of time, trying to deprogram thought patterns and behaviors. The time spent with the child is much more about quality versus quantity.

Example 2
On the flip side, mothers who provide stable homes for their children may have to do some deprogramming as well. The fathers may try to over compensate on their weekends with expensive items, while Mom is viewed as being frugal, because she chooses not to buy the new video game system versus a much needed item. The non-custodial parent can appear to ride in on a white horse with gifts and presents, while the custodial parent seems like the enforcer.

Example 3
When a non-custodial parent with a loose lifestyle of partying and frivolous dating only becomes a parent when their child comes to visit, the father's bachelor lifestyle is bound to show. The child may return from the visit emulating what they saw in terms of their language, behavior and ideologies.

Usually, deprogramming becomes less necessary the more a child understands right from wrong, and has reached an age where they are not as easily influenced.

In this instance, the behavior is "negative" because it is different or unlike the way the normal household runs. One's environment can be very influential on one's attitude. The negative behavior or tone of the other household can be brought back with the child when he or she returns to their custodial parent's home.

When Visitation Is Used Maliciously

Visitation time should not be used as a time to seek revenge, period. Some custodial parents use this opportunity to get back at the non-custodial parent by withholding the child through changing the weekend of visitation at the last minute, cutting the visitation time short, and/or scheduling other events on the non-custodial parent's weekend (time).

An example would be if during a heated argument between two parents, one parent says "Fine. Well Sarah's not coming over this weekend, until you…"
This behavior is a tactic used by parents who actually want the other parent to get fed up and say, "I'll just get them next time!".

When a parent turns away in defeat and doesn't end up seeing their child on that particular weekend, the custodial parent may actually be happy because they got under the non-custodial parent's skin, further validating their own feelings that the non-custodial parent doesn't want to be with the child or won't stand up to them.

Maybe the custodial parent has something planned on their weekend off that the non-custodial parent is aware of, and out of spite, the non-custodial parent suddenly can't come and get the child; which forces the custodial parent to have to change their plans, or forego them altogether. In both examples, the visitation is being used as a form of control, and the main objective of the child being able to spend time with both parents goes out the window, because of the selfishness of the parent(s).

What to Do if You Are Being Denied Visitation

Unfortunately, it is an all-too-common occurrence that some non-custodial parents are denied the right to see their children. When the parents can't work out a schedule of their own, the non-custodial parent must make sure that they have a visitation order in place with their state's court system. Many parents don't realize that they must go through the court system and officially have a visitation order established to assure they can have the legal right to see their child. If you don't have an order in place designating specific times of visitation, the parent withholding the child can claim that they are doing nothing illegal.

If you have an existing court order and your existing order specifies custody/visitation, then you can file a motion to enforce the existing order. Please note the motion must be set in the same court as your existing order (so if the case was previously heard/decided in Georgia, then that's where you have to file now).

Do NOT stop paying child support as this can cloud the issue. Your child's custodial parent can try to use that as a reason as to why they denied visitation (regardless of whether or not they should have done so). Be sure to seek legal advice (if you do not already have an attorney). If you don't have the name of an attorney, contact the State Bar Association (all states have one) and ask for a referral.

Filing Criminal Charges Against the Other Parent

To file a criminal charge against the custodial or parent for interfering with your visitation rights, you should call your local police or county sheriff and file a complaint. Before you do this, make every effort to work it out with the custodial parent. It is unfortunate when it comes to the point where one parent is forced to make such drastic decisions based upon the actions of the other parent. You really don't want to see this happen, but you should also be familiar with the Visitation Interference Law in your state. Whether you decide to handle it this way is completely up to you, and depends on individual circumstance.

Even when some judges hold the custodial parent in contempt for denying mandated visitation, or assign a fine for noncompliance, there is no actual way to enforce the visitation order.

If I Pay Child Support Do I Automatically Have the Right to See My Child?

Unfortunately, the answer is no. Making child support payments does not automatically give a non-custodial parent visitation rights. The non-custodial parent must petition the court for visitation rights.

What Do You Do if the Custodial Parent Always Tries to Create a Confrontation When You Pick Up Your Child?

If it becomes physical with the custodial parent when you are attempting to pick up your child, (with the custodial parent being the initiator), go to your local police station to file a police report. Keep record of the report. Documenting the assault will serve as evidence should you need it for court. Notify the court that you feel unsafe picking up the child from the parent's house, and they will arrange for a neutral pick up/drop off location. Usually, a public place is recommended, with the police station being one of the top choices.

What Do You Do When the Non-Custodial Parent Does Not Abide By the Visitation Order, and Does Not Regularly See Their Child?

The first step would be for the custodial parent to calmly sit down and attempt to talk to the parent about their inconsistencies, or non-existence. In the discussion, the parent will need to point out what it does to the child when they break their promises, and discuss ways to find a solution, i.e. changing the visitation times, etc. This may be very hard for the custodial parent to do, due to the negative emotional feelings towards the non-custodial parent. The parent will have to try to talk about it first to see if the behavior can change.

The non-custodial parent should never be completely denied visitation if they are making attempts, unless the visit could prove to be harmful to the child.

If the father becomes an absent parent, completely drops out of the child's life, or perhaps was never in it, here are some suggestions for coping from family relationship expert Dr. Marilyn Heins, M.D.

Don't Dwell on the Absence Of the Parent
Don't think, "My poor child doesn't have a mother/father. He/she is doomed to a life of unhappiness." The reality is children do survive without a parent with the help of other nurturing family members and love from you.

Emphasize the Positives, and Be Grateful
Think of what your child HAS: a loving, concerned, caring father/mother for starters. Focus on giving your child all that you can as a parent.

Concentrate on Your Child's Strengths
What do they excel in at school? What can they be taught that will give them an edge in this competitive world? Help the child develop competencies based on their likes and talents--music, art, sports, collecting rocks--whatever.
If it is an issue, tell them you understand the void in their life and you wish it could have been different, then explain that the two of you are going to make the best of life together.

They Don't Have to Be Just Another Statistic
Don't assume children have an emotional problem because of the absent parent. It may not bother them as much as you think. You never really know until their actions begin to show what they are actually feeling. Children tend to meet our expectations. Expect yours be happy and successful and they will be!

Don't Overcompensate

Don't fall into the trap of giving a child THINGS to make up for the absent parent. This action can have negative consequences if the child becomes spoiled or begins to adapt to the notion that THINGS = LOVE.

Don't Try to Get a Man/Woman in Your Life to Be Your Child's New Father or Mother

If you meet someone, judge whether this is the one for you, and someone worthy of being a part of your child's life. Don't compound your child's loss of a 24/7 parent by bringing home dates until you are sure there is a committed relationship; kids are not only devastated by subsequent breakups, but they will loose respect for the temporary authority figures.

A child doesn't ask to be put in situations where they must choose between the two people they love the most, or be forced to live two lives. It is we, as parents, that make the decisions that place them in this position, ultimately shaping their lives.

Couples don't always stay together. However, making sure that what the two of you have created gets completely nourished, and grows to be able to fully function on their own, IS your responsibility.

Lighten your children's load.

Make it as painless as possible by cooperating so they will receive benefits from growing with both of you.

A Child's Personal Feelings About The Importance of Visitation

My father and mother divorced when I was just 2 years old, and thus began the cycle of visitation. I would say the time spent with my father was more quality than quantity; more impactful than consistent. Undoubtedly, it has greatly influenced who I am today. Because my father was a truck driver and hauled cars from one end of the country to the other, he would often be out of town for long periods of time. When he would call, he could be anywhere from California to Pennsylvania, which meant I had to see him when he was in town.

My earliest recollection of my visits is when I was about 4. Growing up, I recall going away on what I thought was a long trip; from Detroit to Ann Arbor, Michigan! I now know that the commute was only about a 45 minute drive, but to someone whose longest trip had been going to my grandmother's house and back, the trip felt like a true adventure. When your mother doesn't drive, and you don't have a car, forty-five minutes is like driving from Michigan to Florida!

I lived alone with my mother who became a single parent through divorce. She, along with my grandparents raised me on the Northwest side of Detroit. Between the safety of our neighborhood and my mother's own health challenges, I stayed in the house a lot, which led to the development of my creativity; I basically had to create things to do.

Although my father had a good job, my mother never sought or received any official child support. As much as we struggled to make ends meet, I wish they had arranged something consistent. However, my father always seemed to come in on a white horse to save the day at monumental times. For example, when I was in the fourth grade and decided I wanted to play an instrument, he made the trip to the city to the music store to rent my very first clarinet. As a result of my father investing in my new hobby, I played through my entire school and college years. In fact, it even helped me to receive a music scholarship and travel the world with the greatest college band in the country, Florida A&M University's "Marching 100". He was there financially when I wanted to go to music camp, and visit colleges. And, my father was "there" even to take me down to Tallahassee, Florida for college, as I waved good-bye to my mother in Detroit.

My father grew up on the Eastside of Detroit, where he saw much of his family die to drugs and fighting. When I was younger, my father realized that I was basically a slave to my environment, and decided he would bring me up to Ann Arbor to give me a "different view" of the world. My father didn't want me to grow up being fearful, so he provided an environment where I could explore safely. My dad lived within walking distance of the University of Michigan in downtown Ann Arbor. The streets bustled with young college students, eclectic shops, cool eating places, theatres, and department stores. You name it. It was there. I especially liked the Ann Arbor Art Fair. Then my father would do something I had never experienced; he would pull out a crisp twenty dollar bill and give it to me. That twenty dollars felt like a hundred dollars to me – I felt rich, and I was, in more ways than one.

Visiting the University of Michigan campus made me admire the college kids, and dream of attending college myself. I saw the intensity they had, hustling from one class to the other; plus they looked like they were having fun!
While my mother provided me with class, morals, stability, structure, and spirituality; my father complimented my development with a different skill set; being free, fearless, entrepreneurial, and thinking out of the box. I needed both!

During visits with my father, I saw a new life and reality – a world of possibilities. In fact I became the entrepreneur I am today during those trips. I watched my father write and publish his own magazine and own an antique bicycle store. And he was never without a camera. I actually went on my very first photo shoot with my Dad! How ironic it is that I would have a career in the film and television industry years later!

He exposed me to a host of people of different nationalities and cultures that I would have never seen at my mother's home. My father opened the world beyond Detroit, and his adventures made me reach, becoming a person who was unafraid to take chances in life.

My father had only a few instructions on my visits: "budget your money for the weekend, (for food, entertainment, etc), check in every few hours, and be home before the street lights come on". As soon as I walked out of his cool apartment, I entered a new exciting world, and felt free to explore. The energy from the students made me excited, and I felt like my world was completely open to discovery. There were the shops where I discovered fashion, and eateries where I would have lunch. I could also catch a movie, and then go on the main street where the students congregated. It was the most exhilarating feeling.

Back on Ohio street in Detroit, there was no way I could have been out by myself. Here I was free to explore and learn. Whether my father knew it or not, he gave me the gift of independence. What he also instilled in me was confidence, fearlessness and initiative. He made me an explorer. I realize that those weekends, no matter how few and far between, helped influence the person I am today.

My father also would plan skating outings and take me to visit his friends at their beautiful homes; essentially opening this new world to me during my visits. Although he changed apartments often, he would always stay in really nice places. My most favorite place was Geddy's Lake Townhouses where my brother and I would go fishing right outside his window, and catch big fish too! Going to arcades, spending time on the computer, or watching him be an entrepreneur were all things I would have missed out on had my mother decided to not allow me to have a relationship with my father because of his inconsistent behavior. Although I didn't see my father every other weekend (it was more like a few times a year), those times were meaningful. During those visits I would see my brother and experience another way of living. I often wonder what it would have been like to have spent every other weekend with them both?

When I did visit, I had one expectation; I was going to have a memorable weekend with my father and see my brother. I always knew that anything could happen during those trips! I also saw some things that I probably had no business being exposed to at my age. When I returned home and shared my weekend activities with my mother, anything she felt was negative that happened and was worth mentioning, she would address it separately with my father and keep it moving.

I can't imagine the deficit I would have had my mother decided that she wasn't going to allow me to see my father. In spite of her feelings about his shortcomings, she looked passed my father's inadequacies because she knew in her heart what was best for me. I imagine she probably did a lot of praying back then as she still does today.

My father died years ago, but if he could look at my life today, he would see himself, and the seeds he planted years ago back in that cool apartment in Downtown Ann Arbor.

Opposites attract – and although my parents may not have been good together, they both had things that I needed that made me who I am – the fact is, I needed them both.

That's why my visitation time meant so much to me. It's why I can relate and not be jealous or selfish with my own husband and my stepchildren. I had been in their shoes.

Thanks Ma for being selfless, nurturing, and constant.

Thank you Daddy for having vision when I needed it most.

Brandi Mitchell

Chapter 4
"Hi. My Name Is Child Support"

"And I'd Like To Introduce You To My Friend Of The Court."

The Financial Responsibilities of Raising a Child

Although conceiving a baby may be free, raising and caring for the child is definitely not. Providing for the child is both the mother's and father's responsibility. Consequently, the ability of future parents to contribute to the needs of the child, should always be of primary concern before individuals choose to participate in the "creation" of the child. Whether married or not, parents will spend a minimum of 18 years financially providing for their child, and it will be very expensive.

For example, according to one online calculator, it takes almost $400,000 US Dollars (USD) to raise a child from birth to age 18. Other sources estimate the cost at $250,000 USD or more. For parents who put their kids through college, tuition can add a minimum of fifteen thousand dollars to that estimate per year. Although this may seem like an unaffordable amount of money, keep in mind that the cost of raising children is spread out over almost two decades. Divided equally by 18 years, it will cost you roughly over $22,000 USD per year to raise a child.

The reality of our society today is that nearly forty percent of children are born to unwed parents, who ultimately become single parents. While teenage mothers were at one time the primary sector of the rising rates in unwed births, statistics today show that the steepest increase is among college-educated women and those with professional or managerial jobs. The new group of unwed parents are choosing to have children prior to marriage in non-committed relationships because they are not ready for marriage, or do not have a marriage prospect. This group has the ability to single handedly support and maintain a child. The father is merely a donor and does not actively participate in the life of the child.

When there is no commitment between the parents and/or a lack of financial accountability from the non-custodial parent, the responsibility of providing money for the child will be put entirely on the custodial parent. On the flip side is the custodial parent expecting the non-custodial parent to provide for both the child as well as their personal needs. In the middle of the conflict is the child, who often is used as the bargaining tool between the parents, each with their own agenda.

Although the majority of the stories that we are familiar with tell of the deadbeat dad who won't spend time or money for their child, there is also the other side, where the father really wants to see his child. Unfortunately, in public opinion and in court judgements, he ultimately pays for all of the inaction of the deadbeat dads. Diligent and responsible fathers are rewarded for their attempts to parent their child by constantly being pulled in court by the mother as she tries to get more money, perhaps still denying visitation to the father. The whole ordeal usually vacillates from one extreme to the other as taxpayers and children pay for the parent's choices played out on an emotional battleground.

Who's Your Daddy?

Confirming & Establishing Paternity

*Paternity is defined as the biological
relationship between a father and his child.*

*Establishing paternity is the process
of making that kinship legal.*

Although a very touchy subject, paternity needs to be discussed when there is a question as to who is the actual father of the child. Either the man questions he fathered the child and calls for the test, or the mother initiates the test to prove that the man in denial, is in fact, the father of their child.

Historically, there are numerous cases where men have supported a child they believed to be their biological son or daughter, only to find out later that the child was never theirs. In cases like this, one would expect that the mother would be absolutely sure who is the father of her child. Sadly, this is not always the case. Look at any of your favorite daytime talk shows, and you will find at least one show devoted to hashing out, in front of a TV audience of course, who is Mary's Baby Daddy. Provided as entertainment, this is an all too common occurrence in the real world. Lives are crushed when a family discovers that the child they love belongs biologically to someone else. When the truth is disclosed, other men exhale a sigh of relief when it is proven that the child is not theirs.

The DNA Parentage Test

When the man or woman questions who has fathered a child, they can initiate a DNA paternity test. A DNA paternity test establishes genetic proof of the child's biological father. DNA testing is currently the most advanced and accurate technology to determine parentage. In a DNA parentage test, the probability of parentage is 0 percent if the alleged parent is not biologically related to the child. When the probability of paternity is typically greater than 99.9 percent, the alleged parent is biologically related to the child.

The DNA parentage test can also generate legally admissible results that are used to determine child support, custody, inheritance, social welfare benefits, immigration, or adoption purposes.

Paternity Fraud: "I Wanted Him to Be the Father"

Entered into common use in the late 1990s, Paternity Fraud is the term introduced by fathers' and men's rights activists in situations where a mother names a man to be the biological father of a child, particularly for the purpose of collecting child support (also referred to as child maintenance), when she knows or suspects that he is not the biological father.

Father's rights activists state that in cases of paternity fraud, there are many potential victims: the non-biological father, the child deprived of a relationship with his/her biological father, and the biological father who is deprived of his relationship with his child. Subsidiary victims include the child and extended families on all sides.

In particular, financial hardship can result for the non-biological father and his other children and spouse when the man has been forced to make child support payments for another man's child.

While there are still a large number of men who owe money for the support of their biological children that are definitely theirs, it is also estimated that about 300,000 men each year become a victim of paternity fraud.

Support For Your Child

Working Out Your Own Financial Plan of Commitment

When two parents are no longer together in a relationship, but are mature enough to work out the financial needs of their child, they can bypass the court system and handle the child's care on their own as parents. The parents decide when the payment is to be paid be made (i.e. weekly, bi-weekly, monthly, or in a lump sum). This type of agreement works best when the parents are respectful of each other, and are committed to sharing the financial responsibilities for the needs of their child, despite the fact that they are no longer in a relationship.

If you and your ex work out a financial and custodial plan outside the courts, it is crucial that you have a written agreement that is signed in front of witnesses and notarized. This document will be an asset should your relationship with your ex change or if your ex does not meet the terms of the agreement.

If the parents are still working through their feelings towards each other, they may not be on the best of terms; which makes being rationale and fair almost impossible.

When Things Change

When either of the parents enters another relationship or gets married, one of the parents may want to change the financial plan. If the non-custodial parent was being monetarily generous, which may have covered the mother's personal needs as well, that may change when either parent enters into a committed relationship. The non-custodial parent will focus more on the actual needs of the child, cutting off personal perks to the ex.

When the custodial parent enters a committed relationship, the custodial parent's mate may want a more formal agreement for the money being "given" to their significant other. They may feel that the exchange of money is a form of control over the ex. In either case, the time for a formal agreement may be best for the child. This is where the courts will become an important part of the process.

Child Support

A Child Support Order is a document from a court that states when, how often, and how much a parent is to pay for the financial support of their child. A Child Support Order is typically part of a paternity judgment or a divorce decree.

Child support was established with the belief that children should share in the standard of living of both parents. Courts use a set formula as a basis for calculation. From that number, they modify the amount based on other factors.

> *The Court has the authority to modify the judgment when motioned by either party.*

What the Order Can Solve or Alleviate

• The Child Support Order makes sure that one parent does not carry the entire load of supporting the child. The non-custodial parent will be legally responsible to support their child regularly.

• In cases where the parents officially end an on-again off-again relationship, the child support order stipulates that the court will handle the collection of support and the distribution to the custodial parent. Not only does this cut the financial and emotional ties to the ex, it prevents the child from suffering due to nonpayment, and prevents the custodial parent from undue hardship in pursuing the ex to meet his/her financial obligations. *The focus is then put on the well-being of the child.*

• No Emotional Blackmail – When there is a legal system in place for visitation and finances, the ability of the custodial parent to play controlling, emotional games involving the child and the non-custodial parent is lessened. The non-custodial parent has rights as a parent and an obligation to provide for the child financially through a governing system.

How is Child Support Calculated?

When calculating child support, some states base their calculation only on the income of the non–custodial parent. In other states, both parent's income is taken into consideration. Guidelines for addressing extraordinary living expenses such as college tuition, daycare and extracurricular activities differ by state and parental income.

When determining the amount of child support, all income is taken into consideration. This includes all overtime, bonuses, income from second jobs, commissions, etc. The formula is based on the respective net incomes of the parent(s). Federal and state income taxes, Social Security and Medicare tax, health insurance, union dues and other mandatory expenses are subtracted from a parent's gross income to arrive at his/her net income. The Friend of the Court has the authority to modify the judgment when motioned by either party.

The court ordered support payments are usually scheduled on a monthly basis. Many states now require that child support be paid by wage assignment (automatic deductions from the paycheck weekly) that an employer remits directly to the courts whenever available, thus reducing the need for subsequent enforcement actions.

Components Used In Calculation

- Number of children who are the subject of the pending support action

- Net monthly income of non-custodial parent

- Net monthly income of custodial parent

- Amount of monthly support paid by non-custodial parent for children or spouse from any prior relationships

- Monthly cost of health insurance paid by non-custodial parent

- Monthly cost of daycare paid for by non-custodial parent

- Amount of monthly support paid by custodial parent for children or spouse from a prior relationship

- Monthly cost of health insurance paid by custodial parent

- Monthly cost of daycare paid for by custodial parent

- Provisions for any additional children the non-custodial parent may have.

How Do Childcare Costs Get Factored In?

Because childcare costs are incurred so that a parent is able to earn income, it means that a greater amount of combined income is available for the support of the child. Since both parents benefit from the cost of childcare, this cost is divided between the parents (usually 50 percent each). The parent who actually pays the childcare expense receives payment from the other parent.

Standard of Living Factors

Each parent is supposed to pay for child support according to his or her ability commonly referred to as "circumstances and station in life". A parent with the higher standard of living has the obligation to ensure his or her children share in that lifestyle. However, a non-custodial parent cannot be forced to pay child support beyond his or her means simply to match the custodial parent's new "station in life" (as in the case where the custodial parent remarries into a wealthier social position).

If the Non-Custodial Parent Marries, Is Their Spouse's Income Used to Calculate Child Support Payment Amounts?

Many states, provide that a new spouse's income cannot be considered in the calculations for the support of a stepchild.

Your state may have different rules so do your research for where you live. To ensure financial security, the spouse of the non-custodial parent should set up and maintain separate savings and checking accounts. That way, their funds do not become comingled with the non-custodial parent's funds, and a court, should the question ever arise, will always be able to calculate whose income is whose and where the funds came from. This is important if the non-custodial parent owes back support payments, because the court can seize monies from any bank account bearing the non-custodial parent's name and social security number. This can create financial havoc. If the courts seize the funds, all hope is not lost. The non-custodial parent can petition for half of the money to be credited back to the joint account. If the non-custodial parent is working, it is assumed that at least half of the money is the spouse's.

> *To avoid the spouse's money being seized, the two*
> *should keep separate bank accounts and make*
> *every attempt to stay current with their payments.*

Keep in mind, even if you are successful in petitioning the court to return funds, it is a time consuming process and you may not have the money to pay your bills while you are going through the process.

What Are the Tax Consequences of Child Support?

For Federal Income Tax purposes, received child support payments are not income and are tax-free to the custodial parent.

Unfortunately, the parent who makes the payments cannot deduct the amount as an expense on his or her federal tax return even if they are not allowed to deduct the child as a dependent. Which parent is allowed to use the dependant deduction should be decided when the support order is drafted.

How Long Is the Non- Custodial Parent Required to Pay?

The duration of child support responsibility depends upon state law. All states require both parents to be financially responsible for their child generally through the child's eighteenth birthday if they are in school. A few states have extended the time for financial responsibility beyond the age of 18.

For example, in New York State, you are no longer liable at age 18 if they are no longer in school and are economically independent and working. But the age increases to 21 if the child is in college or still in school.

Emancipation

A child who is emancipated, no longer receives child support.

If the child gets married, reaches the age of 18 or 19, is on active military duty, or if the court orders that emancipation is in the best interest of the child, child support ceases.

The custodial parent can also choose to release the non-custodial parent of their child support order, even if the non-custodial parent owes back support.

The Child Support Order Process

Step 1: Open a Child Support Case

To open a case, either parent can call Child Support Services (CSS) and schedule an appointment. The non-custodial parent must complete an application form and pay an application fee. Applications are available from all CSS offices. You may call any office and ask them to mail you the application or you may access the application on-line. Each states rules are different, therefore seek legal advice. If you do not have the money for a lawyer, contact child services.

Step 2: Locate the Non-Custodial Parent

To obtain or enforce a support order, establish paternity or enforce a support order, the court must know where the non-custodial parent lives and/or works. If possible provide all personal and contact information to the court. It may take several months to get child support if you do not know where the other parent lives or if they are out of state. There is no guarantee the other parent will be found, but the more information you provide, such as the other parent's date of birth and social security number, the easier it will be.

Step 3: Establish Paternity

Before the court will order child support and medical support, paternity must be established. If the parents were not married when the child was born, the biological father can be made the legal father by an administrative or court order. If the man is unwilling to admit paternity, the mother must sign a paternity affidavit before genetic testing and/or a court hearing can be scheduled.

Step 4: File a Support Order

A child support order is established based on the Child Support Guidelines of the state in which you live, and considers the income of both parents and the number of children. Sometimes other factors may be considered.

Step 5: Set up Payment

After a child support order is in place, the support amount will be deducted from the non-custodial parent's paycheck. In most cases state law requires immediate income withholding. This is an easy way for the non-custodial parent to make child support payments and to prevent delays or hardship for the custodial parent. It also provides the non-custodial parent with a record of payments made. If support payments are not deducted from the non-custodial parent's paycheck, they should be paid as directed by the court order. It is very important to keep records and receipts of the payments.

Step 6: Review the Order

Both parents have the right to review a child support order after the order becomes effective. The request must be made in writing to the child support office handling your case. A review may show that the amount being collected or paid is incorrect. Medical insurance, childcare or other financial obligations for the benefit of the child may also be included in the order.

What Happens When The Child Support Is Not Paid?

Enforcing the Support Order and Collecting Arrears

As long as a non–custodial parent remains in the same job nonpayment of child support will not be an issue because their wages will be garnished. If the non-custodial parent changes jobs or becomes unemployed, and either does not pay or makes partial payments, all enforcement action would be necessary.

When a parent does not comply with a support order, they may be found in contempt of court and owe arrearages. Arrearage is when the non-custodial parent owes a past due amount of child support, and the amount continues to build until he or she becomes current. A contempt action may be filed against the non-custodial parent who fails to make support payments or does not fulfill the requirements of the existing child support order. Additionally, until a new order is in place, the non-custodial parent is obligated to pay the full amount of current and past-due support.

There are private and state agencies set up to help a custodial parent pursue a delinquent non – custodial parent. Government agencies have a variety of enforcement tools at their disposal, including:

- Withholding child support from paychecks, unemployment or weekly worker's compensation benefits
- Intercepting federal and/or state income tax refunds
- Reporting parents owing $7,500 or more in child support payments to credit bureaus
- Suspending or revoking driver's, professional or occupational licenses for failure to pay child support
- Reviewing and changing child support orders periodically
- Intercepting lottery winnings of more than $5,000
- Filing contempt of court actions, which may result in a jail sentence if the non-custodial parent is found in contempt of court
- Filing liens to seize bank accounts, lump sum worker's compensation settlements and real or personal property
- Denying, suspending, or revoking the passport of someone who owes more than $5,000 in child support

The Custodial Parent Can Waive Arrears

The custodial parent has the ability to waive the arrears from the non-custodial parent's records by going to the courthouse and requesting that their slate be cleared of the debt. The only person who can request waiver of the arrears is the custodial parent to whom it is owed.

The non-custodial parent may have had a change in their financial status or had no intent of deliberately avoiding paying support, yet because the order is in place, the money owed continues to build astronomically. The non-custodial parent may be upholding all of their parenting duties except this one, and devoting a lot of quality time with their child. The custodial parent may, in turn, feel that the non-custodial parent is entitled to have a fresh start, and therefore, waives the arrears for the non-custodial parent.

Groups That Assist Fathers In Paying Back Support

Fatherhood Programs

The Georgia Fatherhood Program, created by the Office of Child Support Services (OCSS) in 1997, works with non-custodial parents who owe child support through OCSS but are unable to pay. Georgia's Fatherhood Program is the largest state-operated fatherhood program in the country. Over 2,500 non-custodial parents received services through the program in 2009. Gainful, stable employment enables these parents to provide regular financial support payments for their children. Fatherhood Program participants pays $18.7 million each year in child support.

Georgia recognized early on that many non-custodial parents wanted to pay their court ordered child support but lacked the economic capacity to do so. OCSS has partnered with other government and community agencies to develop a comprehensive network of services for this group, and have delivered a successful program.

The Fatherhood Program:

- Generally takes 3 to 6 months to complete

- Serves both fathers and mothers who are non-custodial parents

- Participants are required to work at least 20 hours per week while enrolled in the program

- Participants are required to pay child support during this time

- Upon completion of the program, participants receive assistance in obtaining full-time employment, earning a wage that they can live on, and budget their finances to pay reasonable child support

For information about the Georgia Fatherhood Services Program (www.ocss.dhr.georgia.gov) or similar programs in your state, contact your local Child Support Services office. Applications to most of the programs can be made online.

Modification of Child Support Orders

Significant decreases in income are a valid reason to request modification of your child support order. Before incurring the additional expense of a court-mandated change, one route is to ask the other parent to agree to a temporary reduction or deferral. If successful, put the terms in writing, sign, and date the document, preferably with the advice of a lawyer. This document can be turned into the court as a means to modify the child support amount.

If the ex is not willing to work with you, ask the court to modify the amount of the child support owed in the future, explaining the major, and unavoidable drop in your income. You will also need to clarify that the income is not likely to increase soon, and why the change would be fair and reasonable for both parties. Some judges are sympathetic and receptive to making necessary changes in child support when you have experienced a financial setback. Paying a lawyer for assistance can pay off, especially when you are the non-custodial parent.

You should never refuse to pay child support.

If there are legitimate reasons you are unable to pay, you should petition the court for a modification of your child support obligation. A custodial parent can also petition the court to modify child support if they feel they deserve an increase in monthly payment.

Grounds for Modification May Include:

- A reduction in the income of either parent

- A serious illness or disability of either parent

- A change in your child's circumstances such as reaching the age of maturity or inheriting money

- A change in the financial circumstances of either parent

If something happens (such as temporary layoff), and you want the order modified, do it immediately. If you wait to have the order changed, you will still be required to meet the financial obligations of the original order.

If the custodial parent decides to request a modification in order to receive a payment increase, the difference will be owed to the custodial parent from the time they file for the change, to the time the change is actually granted. This can add up to a lot of money.

Denying Visitation Because of Owed Child Support

Custody and visitation should not be confused with child support.

No state allows a parent to withhold visitation because of unpaid support, or withhold support over visitation disputes. Is there any exception? If the custodial parent disappears for a lengthy time in some courts judges have ruled that the noncustodial parent's duty to pay child support is temporarily suspended, however this is not the norm!

Failure to pay child support is not grounds to stop the right of the non-custodial parent to visit with their child. Visitation is ordered by a court in the best interest of the child to promote love, affection and stability. Visitation is vital to the development and maintenance of a meaningful relationship between child and parent.

Unless the courts order otherwise, the custodial parent must continue to allow visitation with the child despite failure of the non-custodial parent to pay child support.

What if the Custodial Parent Receiving Child Support Does Not Use the Money For the Child's Benefits?

This is a very difficult issue to resolve. On one hand, the custodial parent has the right to spend child support money received as they see fit, in the best interest of the child. On the other hand, the custodial parent has the obligation to provide for the best interests of the child. If the custodial parent is irresponsible in meeting their parental responsibilities toward the child, and the child's needs are not being met, they could be charged with child abuse or neglect. In extreme cases, this abuse or neglect would be grounds upon which a change in custody, in addition to a change in the obligation to pay child support, would be proper.

If you can prove that the custodial parent is wasting the money on things for themselves or has a drug or alcohol problem, you may have a case. You will need documented proof.

Perception is not always reality. Child support is also spent in invisible things- rent, utilities, insurance, etc. While it is normal to expect to see the money spent on tangible items (food, clothes, and activities), if the custodial parent is not bringing in sufficient money to pay the living expenses, your support will go to invisible needs first.

Make Sure That the Custody Order is Correct and Current

*It is critical when permanent changes in custody occur,
the person taking on the custodial role files the required
paperwork with the court system.*

If a child who was living with the mother now lives with their father, the father will have to officially go to the courts to have the custody order changed, stating that they have assumed the role of custodial parent. If the order is not updated, any child support order in place would still be in effect. The father could unknowingly be charged for nonpayment of support; even when the child may have lived with him for years and the parent's reached a verbal agreement.

Other Ways of Using the Support Money

What if the custodial parent is earning a good income and the money received from the non-custodial parent is not a necessity. Here are a few suggestions of how the money can be utilized for the benefit of the child: a savings account, college fund, summer camp, educational trips, sports leagues, extra curricular activities, holiday or gift shopping monies, investment funds (IRA, etc), life insurance, or savings for a car. The point is that the money should be used to benefit the child and not as extra income for the custodial parent.

Quality Time Spent vs. Money, Which One is More Important?

Although money is a necessity for survival, nothing can replace the quality time and love that comes from a parent. Money seems to pale in comparison to the richness of love. There are those who may have very little to offer financially to their children, yet they provide their children with a wealth of life skills, love, attention, and hope. People can end up in strange stations in life where their financial situations may not be as secure and stable as they need to be, causing a temporary financial hardship. Even when parents are married, one or both parents can fall on bad times. What is more important is that what they do have, they share with their children, and their children, in turn, are some of the richest children in the world. One should never confuse child support payments with the parenting of a child. Although financially providing and parenting walk hand-in-hand, money does not make a relationship. If you think it does, how many times have you shared a meal or a day with your banker or the person who signs your paycheck? With the right tools, wealth can be acquired; but the morals, ethics, stability, and character that are the products of sound supportive parenting cannot be bought.

Chapter 5
Why The Drama With The Baby Mama?

What Exactly is a "Baby Mama?"

It Depends on How You Define Yourself

We've all heard it and may be experiencing it. You guessed it - baby mama drama and deadbeat baby daddies. Whether you have been dating someone who has children, or are the one dishing out the chaos, "the drama" is an all too common occurrence in this day in time. If you haven't been in an actual situation with the drama, then you definitely have witnessed it secondhand from friends, relatives, and coworkers. From being taken back and forth to court for more child support to nagging phone calls, endless arguments, lies, and manipulative games; all of it spells drama. Primarily, it is young men and women who are having children long before they have developed any plan for their life or have reached a level of maturity required for successful parenthood.

Additionally, since the trend is that men and women are getting married later, they are not necessarily wiser, and are experiencing the same drama that was once associated only with their younger counterparts.

Drama associated with the baby's mama and daddy occurs between parents when they are no longer together and one or both of them wants to make the other "pay" for their misery. The misery is a result of the failed relationship, ill feelings towards the other parent, or just being unhappy with their current life status. Their unhappiness translates into immature actions, both physical and verbal; which are fueled by anger, hurt, and in some cases ignorance. Ignorance in that they simply don't know or understand that their behavior whether warranted or not, directly effects their own child, as well as block the progression they personally need to go on with their lives. While some of the behavior of the baby mama and baby daddy is learned behavior from their environment, other behaviors that are part of "the drama" boil down to an individual's character and personality.

The more ambitious baby mamas use the bearing of a child as an opportunity to advance financially or socially. The drama goes to an entirely new level if one of the parents decide to commit to a serious relationship with someone else, or dare I say – get married. This is usually when the custodial parent suddenly wants more money or feels the non-custodial parent needs to spend more time with the child.

The drama steps into high gear when the baby mama withholds the visitation rights. The baby mama and baby daddy are very selfish, as their actions are based on hurt feelings and anger, and all the drama is not in the best interest of the child. Sadly many baby mamas feel justified by their actions and fail to see that the big loser in the game is their own child.

The terms have even hit mainstream where reporters and writers refer to a person as "their baby mama" or her new "baby daddy". In fact, I would say that we are ignorant or have become quite desensitized to the terms original meaning and how the label was used to define a parent's insignificance.

Single Mother = Baby's Mama? Not Necessarily.

Some would argue that a single mother and a baby's mama are one in the same, since the end result is that neither is with their child's parent. However, there are differences between those who are raising their child as a single parent and baby mamas and daddies. The biggest factor is the way in which the parent acts when relating with their child's mother or father and centers around their attitude and maturity. In essence, the way they behave in their life with the baby and the child's parent will ultimately dictate which name they deserve.

Baby Mama and Baby Daddy Defined

Baby Mama - *UrbanDictionary.com defines a Baby Mama as the mother of your child(ren), whom you did not marry and with whom you are not currently involved.*

The lack of a stable long-term relationship with the child's parent may lead to bouts of jealousy, and anger that result in baby mama drama.

Another definition could be an unmarried woman who is raising their child out of wedlock. They act immaturely, selfishly, and commit deliberate acts of foolishness towards the child's father, and significant others. The child could be a product of a purely sexual relationship which is unlike that of an ex-wife or girlfriend.

"Oh her? She's nothing to me, she's just my Baby Mama".

The baby mama may act out negatively because of missed child support payments, unfulfilled promises by the father, or by engaging in ongoing convenient sex with the father with no commitment promised.

Baby Daddy - *The Oxford English Dictionary defines Baby Daddy as "the father of a woman's child, who is not her husband or current or exclusive partner."*

The term baby daddy is said to have its roots in Jamaica. The Oxford English Dictionary lists baby-daddy and baby-mama as "colloquial, chiefly African-American" variants of the Jamaican terms baby-father and baby-mother; its first citation for baby-mother hails from the Kingston Daily Gleaner in 1966. It is said that the terms probably arose in Jamaican Creole where they would have been pronounced "biebifaada" and "biebimada"— before taking hold in standard Jamaican English.

On the island, your baby-mother or baby-father is typically someone with whom you are no longer romantically involved.

In Jamaica, if you called your husband your "baby-father," he might be insulted - the term suggests biological fatherhood in the absence of any real parenting.

The Baby Mama & Baby Daddy Become Famous!

The Media and Other Societal Influences

They say that art imitates life. If so, then the popularity of the baby mama/baby daddy in the media and Hollywood has become an extension of the everyday person's life; minus the money and notoriety.

The baby mama/baby daddy label has been catching on for awhile. An Atlanta rap group popularized the term with the 1997 hit My Baby Daddy. Fantasias' song Baby Mama, has become somewhat of an anthem for baby's mamas, and caught flack from critics for being a song that sensationalizes teen parenthood. More recently the group All for One came out with an anthem for men being denied visitation rights entitled Let Me See My Child. On stage, plays such as Baby Mama Drama are making their way around the urban theater circuit. It has even hit the big screen with the films Baby Daddy and Baby Mama. In New York, 300 couples vied for one of 10 all-expenses-paid weddings; a day that organizer and Brooklyn author, Maryann Reid, has dubbed 'Marry Your Baby Daddy Day'.

In a time where bloggers, entertainers and public figures have become our role models of choice, we also see the baby mama and baby daddy trend as an acceptable form for having children outside of marriage within Tinsel town.

The word is used often when speaking of someone's significant other who just happens to be "having my child", when marriage seems to be an "option" for them. Every day, children are being born into homes where one parent will take on a majority role, raising them alone. Society tends to look down on unwed mothers and single fathers. Yet, when we see people that we admire doing the same thing while making it look "fabulous", it creates a false reality that accepts it as just another way of life. What young men, and women don't see are all the nannies, assistants, and financial assets or resources that lightens the parenting load and provide social acceptance and opportunities for the children.

Despite money or fame, we are all human, which means we all feel, hurt, get angry, and have to decide how we handle the cards we are dealt in life. The biggest difference is that unlike some celebrities, most will have no nanny; and your life will be turned upside down when you bring a new life into the world that you must care and support. And when you are doing it alone, or with a lot of drama, nothing is glamorous about that!

I Can Be Your Baby Mama, But NOT Your Wife? OK

Often, male celebrities who attain some measure of success, bring their baby's mama(s), and their drama along with them in their rise to stardom. When some celebrities run as far away from the baby's mama as possible; this only fuels more anger. Successful men are seen as prime targets for the "drama" because they seem like a good pay day should a child result from their intimate escapades; no matter how brief. Girlfriends of these public figures remain in the baby mama status, progressing with no change in marital status. Only the strong and diligent make it to the status of wife. Unfortunately, the majority of them never quite make that walk down the aisle. Public figures, due to their visibility and influence, can unconsciously send a message that it's alright to be with the baby's mama and not commit. This further validates what the everyday person is experiencing in their own reality. Despite having children with these men, the reality many of these women face is that they gain no legal relationship commitment outside the financial relationship that meets the needs of the child. This is the reason the child becomes the biggest manipulation tool either parent has.

Repeat Offenders

There are those baby mamas and daddies that have children with multiple partners, ending up with more than one baby mama/ baby daddy. In this regard, they haven't learned from the first baby experience. Instead, they continue to have children in relationships that will end up nowhere. Men, more so than women, have more children as they can impregnate women simultaneously, often overlapping and celebrating multiple birthdays in one month! Since the woman has to bear the child, it slows her down nine months. There are still women however who manage to end up with two, or more fathers of their children.

Down the road, if the mother or father marries, the adjustment will be no small undertaking, as each of their children has to develop a relationship with their separate fathers or mothers as well as have to relate to each other as siblings.

Double your drama, double your pain.

Acceptance of the Title

Women especially, have seemed to accept the title, further perpetuating a behavior that unconsciously conveys to men that it is acceptable to father children without making a long-term, or legal commitment. The fact that so many people embrace the terms baby mama and baby daddy shows a shift has occurred amongst American values. To willingly adopt the baby mama/ baby daddy title as if it were a badge of honor shows acceptance and desensitizing in America in the aspect of the responsibilities of parenthood.

Even more bizarre is that women and men willingly assign themselves the title, most unaware of its meaning. They have accepted the baby mama title as an "acceptable" behavior.

I realized during my research for this book that many people used the baby mama/baby daddy title, but in fact had varying opinions about the meaning of the word. Some mature women accepted the title. Along with their acceptance, they also to some degree "played out" its role, reverting to immature and out of character tendencies that did not reflect their current life. Emotionally driven, these women mimicked themselves at a younger age when they were with the father of their child, those emotions causing their immature antics. Even middle-aged parents seemed to step into a kind of time warp when relating to and dealing with their child's other parent becoming a completely different person.

Mis Labeled

I also found women due to societal influences who called themselves baby mamas, when in all actuality, their behavior did not classify them as such. These women were responsibly raising their children as single mothers, and avoiding the 'drama'. The women didn't realize that using such a word themselves was negating their role as a single parent. They basically were perpetuating a popular phrase that has become a mutant form of motherhood.

It is my opinion, if you change the power behind the baby mama/daddy movement, those titles will not have the influence and notoriety that they receive. If people can see that once you have stepped into the role of the parent, you automatically have to place the child's needs first. Everything you do, will be reflected by your child. This accountability may allow them to make better choices, and avoid the whole drama route associated with baby mamas and baby daddies.

Now, why would you want to call yourself a Baby Mama again?

A Deeper Look: Generational

Some people are already the third generation of baby mamas and baby daddies. They may have seen their grandmother and mother being baby mamas. Now they have added to the cycle themselves by having children outside of marriage and being an initiator of the drama. If they are not working towards raising their child different, the whole stigma could be passed to a fourth generation. Unconsciously, drama mamas demonstrate through their actions how to "act" when dealing with the baby's daddy. Because they have seen and observed first hand the behavior of those closest to them, it seems like a natural course of action to bring children into this environment. It will take stepping up by desiring a different life or being exposed to new influences, to avoid the vengeful and draining path.

Men who may have been abandoned or have never known their fathers, many times duplicate the same behaviors. Those who are emotionally secure do the complete opposite, actively participating in their children's life to give them what they never experienced.

Sometimes It Boils Down To: Poor Choices + Immaturity + Anger Create Baby Mamas And Baby Daddies

Philosophy (or what lies) behind the anger of Baby Mamas

When we think of the whole process of having a child; the doctor's visits, body and hormonal changes, life adjustment, and added emotional and financial responsibilities, bringing a child into this world is a significant undertaking. For the mother, the connection and feelings that come along with creating a child are enough to make her want to form a family with her child's parent. This is especially true if the relationship is based on legitimate feelings that one or both partners experienced prior to conception.

When the initial excitement of having the baby has worn off, it is not unusual for the other parent's involvement to become slow or non-existent. If the relationship turns sour, the mother may feel cheated, disillusioned, and left with the reality that she will be primarily raising the child alone. The mother will harbor resentment, and look for ways to adjust her life. The mother who accepts the responsibility will begin to carve out a life for her and her newborn. The alternate route is the baby mama route, where she becomes vengeful, angry, and vindictive. While it is natural to feel resentment for the absentee father, what must also be considered is that when the two people consented to having sexual relations, they both knew there was a possibility that they could have a baby. Women have to make good decisions about their lives because they are wired to be attached to the child from the beginning, and must face the reality that they may end up being both mommy and daddy based on their choices when they had sex.

If the mother cared for the father at all, and the relationship did not work, she will constantly be reminded of him through the eyes of the child, even if the father is not present in the child's life.

What's at the Root of the Behavior of the Baby Mama's and Baby Daddies?

- Selfishness
- Emotional Immaturity
- Anger & Jealousy
- Fear

The Different Types of Baby Mamas

The following paragraphs define multiple scenarios that give birth to the Baby Mama drama. You may find that some women will overlap categories.

One-Night Stand

The One-Night Stand Baby Mama earns her title from the event of a sexual encounter taken place on a one-time occasion. If she is promiscuous, she may have another child or children that have multiple baby daddies. If this is the One-Night Stand Baby Mama's first child, she has been playing this game with her life many times, only this time she is unhappy because the baby was not part of her plan.

Beneficial/Opportunistic

The Beneficial and Opportunistic Baby Mama is a gold digger. She realizes what is to be gained (money and/or status), and knowingly plans on her pregnancy as a way of "securing" her future. The Beneficial Baby Mama is found in every social structure from the innocent young neighborhood girl, to the savvy, sophisticated woman who targets NBA players and celebrities.

The Concept Is The Same, Baby = Pay Day!

Disillusioned/Woman Scorned

The Disillusioned or Woman Scorned Baby Mama may have had promises of marriage or been in what she thought was a serious relationship, only to find out that the man was seeing other women, only wanted sex from her, or that he had no plans to marry her.

"I thought we were going to be together when we decided to have this baby" repeats in her head. These women have been completely deceived. She is now scorned and broken, choosing to let her hurt guide her interaction with the father.

Commitment Driven

The Commitment-Driven Baby Mama has been in a relationship with a man that she sensed was coming to an end, but she doesn't want to be without him. In an attempt to keep her ties to the man and salvage their relationship, she purposely gets pregnant thinking "This will keep them with me". When the plan doesn't work, and he doesn't want her, she will make his life miserable. She hopes that by their child connection, she will have a chance to bring him back to an intimate and permanent relationship.

The Commitment-Driven Baby Mama will especially act up when the father dates other people. If the father gets married, she will be the one who needs emotional counseling due to her feelings of inadequacies that make her question "Why not me?", "Wasn't I good enough?".

Jekyll and Hyde
The Jekyll - Hyde Baby Mama appears to be one person to the father before having the baby, but after the baby is born, becomes unrecognizable. To her child's father, she may have even seemed like Mrs. Right! From her point of view, when seeing the actions of other baby mamas, the Jekyll-Hyde Baby Mama vows that she "would never act in that kind of way with her child or baby's father if things went wrong". Because she has not been in the situation before, she actually emulates the exact behavior she once despised. The Jekyll - Hyde Baby Mama could be educated, and very composed, yet she doesn't quite know how to deal with her anger. As a result, she acts out of character, losing control of her true identity. The baby's father finds himself saying, "How did I ever connect with her? I can clearly remember the days of bliss when she was the most beautiful person. I never thought she was capable of what she has become."

The Drama That Comes with the Baby Mama
When it comes to "baby mama drama", there are different levels that occur from slightly irritating events to extremely dangerous

physical activity. The extent of what can be encountered as the recipient or "target" of the drama may include manipulative games where the child is the tool or 'weapon-of-choice', to physical altercations, all which sabotage the relationship between the father and child.

The Baby Mama's personality will determine your punishment!

Just how long does the drama last?
How long the drama from the baby's mama lasts varies. To accept that there will most likely be some type of conflict, would be realistic thinking when added to the fact as time passes, other children and spouses will become a part of the scenario.

Time plays a great factor in leveling the drama as the maturing of the individuals involved helps the parents to develop responses more adult-like. The person administering the drama usually lowers the fury level when they find happiness, or accept the fact that the intimate part of their relationship has no future. Unfortunately, there are men and women who choose to hold on to their ill feelings even as their child reaches adulthood and the other parent has "grown up" and matured. For these stubborn men and women, all that remains is anger. They still bad-mouth the other parent to their child, even when there is no relationship between the non-custodial parent and child.

The 5 Year Rule

I found this rule to be true when dating or marrying someone who has children five years of age or younger. In the 5 Year Rule, if the child between separated parents is five years of age or younger, the relationship is still "fresh" and therefore, the feelings are also "fresh" between the parents. Realize that there may be extra drama, because chances are there are many feelings still circulating around the parents and their former relationship. Also there has to be more interaction with the parents because the child is so young, and there are many first occurrences and milestones (like walking, speaking, schooling, doctors visits, etc.) that both parents will be dealing directly with each other.

Another thing to consider is they may have had a live-in or dating relationship and sexual encounters after the child was born, up to the time when they formed a relationship with you!

This makes it extremely difficult when forming new relationships. Suddenly all ties and occasional flings are cut, because if the male finally finds "the one" he wants to settle down with, the true "drama" begins.

The 5 Year Rule Quiz

When dating or considering marrying someone who has a child five years old or younger, both of you should take this quiz to determine if the relationship is fully dissolved, and how much baby mama/baby daddy drama you can expect should you proceed.

The Five Year Rule Quiz
(To be asked to the parent that you are dating or marrying)

1. How long have you and the parent of your child been separated?

2. Why are the two of you not together?

3. Who initiated the break up?

4. If you didn't marry, did you ever intend to get married? Why didn't you?

5. When was the last time there was any sexual contact?

6. Was your child planned?

7. Have there ever been any questions of paternity? Has she ever insinuated that the child may not be yours

(if quiz is being given to a male)? If so, did you take a paternity test?

8. How often do you see your child?

9. What type of custody do you have, and do you ever have problems seeing your child(ren)?

10. When you visit your child, is it with your ex, or at your own home?

11. After reading the types of baby mamas defined in this chapter, which one do you think most describes your situation?

Once you hear the answers to the questions, it will allow you to have background info on what type of drama to expect should you decide to get involved and/or marry the individual. Getting as much history about the past relationship will help to understand the current status of the relationship between the parents.

For the Man Experiencing the Drama

For men that receive tons of drama, this quiz is especially enlightening. It provides a way to dissect and reflect on their past relationships. If they personally committed any wrong-doings they have the opportunity to accept responsibility for their actions. If the wrong-doings are still relevant, accepting responsibility and apologizing may reduce your drama. Do it with true sincerity.

Being truthful and sincere is the key.

Women can sense when a man is being sincere a mile away. The time-frame in which the apology is initiated will be completely up to the father. Remember, when people are hurt, they have to be ready to receive and forgive. If the other parent is not ready to receive the apology, it could fall on deaf ears.

Timing is everything.

The Failed Expectations of the Relationship May Be a Driving Force Behind the Drama

The way in which the baby mama/baby daddy relationship dissolved and their current interactions is an indicator of how they will respond when someone new comes in the picture. If you are walking into a drama-filled relationship, pay close attention to how your potential mate has handled the past relationship with his ex(s). It could indicate what you will experience in your future relationship, if it is primarily character flaws.

There are cases when the parents were both young and immature and have since grown from the individuals they were while together. In such cases, it can be expected that some of the anger experienced by the baby mama/baby daddy may have been warranted.

In all actuality, no one should ever allow anyone to have so much power over them that they can not control how they act, respond to, and handle "life".

Situations You Can Encounter When Dealing With Baby Mama Drama

Being Vindictive, What It's Really Saying

In the case of baby mama drama, one thing is for sure, when you are happy with yourself and your life, you have little time or energy to be spent raising havoc in someone else's life. Does the old saying "misery loves company" sound familiar? The vindictive baby's mama appears when the person who is doing the dirt is unhappy, jealous, and still has feelings for the other person. Being vindictive can be a part of the person's nature. This type of behavior is a result of wanting to see someone else who is happy, be as unhappy as they are.

It requires a lot of energy and time to be upset with someone and retaliate. Vindictive behavior also causes stress which reeks havoc on the mind and body. If you are in a romantic relationship with someone else, and being vindictive towards your child's parent, it will put stress on your current relationship and make the person you are currently with question where your heart is. Not moving on is a deterrent to all the things that lie waiting for you, with or without the person you are being vindictive too.

Using Your Child as a Manipulation Device

When parents are no longer together, the child becomes the only connection between the parents, thereby being the only thing that is "negotiable". The child can be used as a tool of manipulation, because aside from the fathers' money, the child is the only way to effect the father.

The sad truth is that most parents who use their child in this way don't even realize they are doing so. But, in the baby's mama case, she is very aware! Mother's don't realize when they say "No, you can't see them, or "If you don't pay me this, you can't see him or her", they are really belittling the value of their child, and negating the child's' right to have both parents in their lives.

Up, Up, and Away! Going Up on Child Support "Just Because"

Even though we have touched on this earlier, because it is done so often, it needs to be restated.

Child support should be determined by the needs of the child in terms of school, clothing, food, activities, and normal shelter.

I think that it is unfortunate when custodial parents increase child support just because they can and want more, or even better, as a way of getting back at the parent. The custodial parent can request an increase in the child support for any number of reasons, even if they aren't valid: the other parent has a love interest, or seems to have advanced (has a new car, goes on a vacation, or changes addresses). A request of this type may be cleverly worded so it appears that the increase is based on need when in fact, it is because the relationship has been completely severed.

The custodial parent should determine the child's needs (not theirs), before they decide to request more money "just because". Along with the legitimate needs of the child being met, more consideration should be taken into making sure the father has a relationship and quality time spent with their child.

"It's Not Your Baby Anyway!"

Every woman knows that telling a man who actually cares about a child that he or she may not be his, is one of the lowest blows anyone can give. On the other hand, for men who intend to be in the deadbeat hall of fame, this is their time to flip cartwheels down the middle of the street through incoming traffic! Telling this to a man who loves his child is a tactic to make the father question paternity, and/or serve as an underhanded attempt to make the father exit the child's life. If the mother was unsure, she may have picked the man that she thought would be a better father, or the one who had the most money. Not only is it a horrible game to play with any man, it really makes the mother look bad to have multiple paternal possibilities.

When a mother makes the father question paternity, the father has two choices:

1) have a paternity test done to prove or disprove it, or

2) omit having the paternity test, and raise the child regardless.

If the father decides that the results of the paternity test won't matter, he may want to make sure he is legally placed as the child's parent so that he can have the rights of a father (should the baby's mama decide she wants to revoke his paternity privileges).

When Did Being a Baby Mama Become a Career Option?

There are some baby mamas that have decided that they should receive enough income from the father's child support to literally support them and all of their children. This means she chooses not to work or has multiple children of whom the mother is receiving support from all the daddies! For example, if the baby mama has three children, from three different men who make a decent living, she could receive $400 - $1000 or more per month per child, (and that's on the low end). The mother could also have under-the-table money coming in and make a decent living off of ALL her babies' daddies.

Liar, Liar! When the Baby Mama Lies to the Child About the Parent and There Intents

In an attempt to taint the image of the father, the baby mama may lie and insinuate to the child that the father does not want to see them, or does not care about them. Usually this happens when the mother hates the father so much that she doesn't want the child to have a relationship with their father, not because the father doesn't want to see his child. The baby mama will then do everything in her power to deny visitation and ensure the child has a poor image of their father. If the father gets married, and begins to have other children, the baby mama will imply to the child that "he has a new family now", thereby insinuating that he doesn't need the child. This is one of the most selfish tactics a baby mama can do, because she has denied her child a piece of themselves.

No Respect

The baby mama may at times talk poorly about the father to the child out of her anger or hurt. Regardless of how much she despises the father, children should be taught to love and respect both parents, whether or not they are worthy. A child should not be put in the middle having to choose between the love and presence of their parents. Assure your child that you both love them and that will never change. Keep your children out of your adult squabbles.

Punishing the Child Because the Parent Is Not Around

"Sometimes if the father is a deadbeat father,
when the child does something wrong,
the mother will constantly remind
the child that they are "just like their father".

The mother's words are actually shaping the child's reality regardless if the statement is true or not. Mother's words are so powerful and creative in nature that she has the ability to cultivate or destroy her child's future.

Some women will even have resentment for their child if they resemble the father. Whenever she looks at the child, she sees the reflection of the man she hates.

When there are siblings who may have multiple fathers, the children may be treated differently based on the feelings associated with the child's father.

Let's Get Physical: The Angry Baby Mama

When people are angry, they sometimes don't know how to control or channel the anger. In the case of a hurt parent, sometimes the only way they can release anger is by physically hurting their ex or his property.

The Angry Baby Mamas will instigate and provoke duels with the baby's father or anyone else who is in their path of rage. If the baby's father has a girlfriend, or even worse a wife in their life, the angry baby mama may want to deliberately start a fight with the "new woman" in her ex's life. The Angry Baby Mama doesn't care if the girlfriend or wife is involved in their disagreement or not. By default they want to physically harm their ex and his love interest. They never stop to consider that the new wife may be a mother just as they are or the image they are conveying to their children. Unfortunately, some angry baby mamas get exactly what they are asking for if they meet up with the wrong "new woman", and an actual confrontation takes place with the new woman.

When faced with an Angry Baby Mama, a man should never respond physically. If the man feels that the potential for a physical confrontation is the inevitable, than he should arrange a meeting place through the courts to see his child or meet in a place where she will not easily be able to 'act out', such as the police station.

For the Angry Baby Mama, the best thing she can do for herself and especially her child is to seek help in dealing with her anger. More than likely, anger issues with the father are an expression of frustration over other problems in her life. If the baby mama is uncontrollable, a restraining order can also be placed on the baby mama, as well as police reports filed in an attempt to protect the father and his loved ones. If the baby mama's actions are such that the father is legitimately concerned about the welfare of his child, the father may request custody of the child.

The Biggest No-No: Child Abandonment

Some baby mamas decide that they don't want to care for their child full-time any more, and the father is suddenly faced with a child on his doorstep, literally. There was a time, when no matter how bad times got for the mother, giving the child up was unimaginable.

There are a growing number of women who are willingly choosing to give up their children for their own selfish reasons. Some baby mamas choose men, partying lifestyles, or careers over raising their child. In these cases, the mothers actually find themselves being the non-custodial parent, or even deadbeat moms. They only assume the parenting role when it's convenient. If the father is not an option for caring for the child, the woman's mother, sister, or grandmother can become the surrogate for the mother.

How Can The Baby Mama Change?

Take Responsibility For Your Actions

It takes two people to make a baby, period! Regardless of whether the father is doing his part or not, you have to take responsibility for your own actions and your own happiness. In order to shift the focus, you will have to stop blaming the father of the child for your current life. Instead, take a realistic look at your life and determine what you would like to change. What would it take for you to actually be happy? What will need to be done to make sure that you and your child are taken care of? These answers can not be found just by adding a man to the equation.

You have to be a whole person before you can
truly have a relationship with a whole man.

Your Number One Priority: Make Yourself a Better Person First

Work on you and your family first. Take inventory, and begin to shape the life you desire for you and your child. If it's returning to or finishing school, there are several options to explore, even if you have to begin on a part-time basis or enroll in online courses. If it's finding yourself spiritually, look for a place of worship where you can grow which will impact your entire family's life.

Develop a game plan, and begin to see the world,
not as the victim, but as the victor!

If Needed, Change Your Atmosphere. Leave Negative People, Places, and Ways of Thinking Behind

Once you have created a plan for your life, make sure your atmosphere is conducive to the growth you expect. Don't keep hanging around all your baby-mama-drama friends who are still in the drama mindset. Don't place yourself back into positions that may have you associated with baby-making men, or dead-end relationships. When dealing with your child's father during times where conflict can arise, choose to handle the situation maturely and in the best interest of your child.

Break the Cycle! Don't Keep Having a Sexual Relationship with the Father or Other Men If Another Baby May Occur

Continual intimate relationships are an emotional tether.

When the relationship is over, it's over! If a man is not marriage material after your baby arrives, future sex is not going to magically make him commit. Doing so always keeps you living in the past, and you may find yourself pregnant again. Don't keep positioning yourself as another man's baby mama. Instead, strive to be a good mother, and a better woman.

Create Your Own Income. Don't Expect the Father to Support Your Entire Livelihood

While I believe men should support their children, I also think that it is important for mother's to make their own money, and model a life of success and work ethic for their children. You want your children to see a positive example that they can duplicate in their own lives. If you show them that you live and depend on someone else for your livelihood, that will become acceptable. If they see that their mom is also working to provide, it sends a message that the mother is productive and someone that the child can admire.

Speak Life to Your Child and Your Circumstance

Embrace your child and create the best life for your family. Regardless of what others may expect, create the life you want for your family. Even if the father is absent or speaks from a negative prospective about the child, speak positively about your child and their future. You will allow your child to have a different outlook on life than they could have ever had with you existing as an angry baby mama.

Once You Are Healed, Don't Accept the Baby Mama Title

Although you are the mother of a baby, don't allow yourself to be referred to as a baby mama. To do so, is accepting this as your reality. Be a loving mother who is determined to be a good role model for your child. Being a baby mama should no longer be a "cute phrase" you should refer or answer to, or one that you perpetuate. Once you feel confident in your "new identity", pick another woman and help her know who she is and where here responsibility lies. Be part of the mission to make baby mama no longer a popular title.

Chapter 6
When Good Dads Get Bad Raps

Hell Hath No Fury Like a Woman Scorned....

Most of the complaints that we hear relating to men and their children from previous relationships, is about the father's lack of responsibility. Often, they refer to the men as deadbeat dads; a term defined as fathers who don't financially support their children. There are many negative stereotypes, from deserting the child's mother which causes her to raise the child alone, all the way to the man that goes around making babies without "fathering" any of them.

When people hear that a man is not married to the mother of their child, they automatically think they are one of the "no good men" who fall into the "deadbeat" category. While there are many men who fit this description, there are also many fathers that really do want to have relationships with their children, supporting their children financially and emotionally. Some of these fathers may not have all of the resources but make up for what they lack financially with the time and effort they put into helping raise their children.

It's a bit of a Catch 22. On one side, you have the fathers who don't work to have relationships with their children where the mother rallies to bring them closer to their children. On the flip side, is the father who really wants to have a relationship with their child, who may get the opposite- the mother who gives them a hard time while working to establish the relationship, and blocks their efforts because she knows he wants to be with his child.

Often, after the bitterness that accompanies a dissolved relationship, the mother harnesses her hatred and hurt for the father by transferring her own pain to the father. One of the most common forms of revenge is denying the father access to their child. The mother will use the relationship with the father and the child to seek revenge or cause pain.

Completely loosing sight of the child's best interest, the mother becomes very self-centered, often justifying her actions with the excuse that the father is not a good father. In the mother's eyes, "he's not paying enough money" or "he's not spending enough time", becomes favorite phrases to justify their actions and dislike of the father.

The reality is that the father really can't win because the tool in which the mother is measuring the father's parenting abilities is skewed and biased; being judged more so by if the man was a good mate, boyfriend, or sometimes even husband, as opposed to a good father.

The biggest loser in the entire situation is the child, as they feel the negative effects of a dysfunctional relationship where they are in the middle. These fathers usually catch it the worse, as the more they try, the more they get knocked down by a system and stereotype carried by the majority that effects even the good fathers who are innocent.

Many men live in a never-ending, continual battle of conflict between the mother of their child and themselves. It shouldn't and doesn't have to be that way. Every man who desires to have a healthy relationship with his child should be allowed to pursue that relationship if the end result is in the child's best interest. Let's examine some of the things fathers have to deal with in pursuing a relationship with their children, and some tips to help them gain access to a being an active part of their children's lives.

Being Denied Visitation

Denying the father the opportunity to visit their child is a form of control that the mother uses to either get what she wants, or for spite. The mother knows that she has little power over the man, so she uses something that is close to the man's heart to achieve a demented sense of empowerment. With no other connections to the ex besides the child, the child now becomes the only form of manipulation by which the mother can use to irritate, get what she wants, or just bring confusion to a perfectly good day.

A lot of parents choose to put a visitation order in place that states the terms by which the non-custodial parent can see their child. Even when there is a visitation order in place, the mother may still refuse to allow the father to see the child, violating the terms of the visitation order without receiving any immediate punishment. I wonder what would happen if every time the mother denied visitation, she would not receive her child support payment. Would it make her a bit more understanding then? Just a thought.

The Most Common Tactics Used In An Attempt To Deny Visitation

Tactic 1
The Mother Could Constantly Change the Pick Up Time of The child, or Cut the Visitation Time Short

The mother commonly gives excuses as to why the child cannot visit the father, citing activities the child has to attend, visiting another relative, their own personal schedule conflict, vacation plans, etc. Under normal circumstances, prior commitments (such as scheduled visitation with the non-custodial parent), should take precedence over other events that may arise.

If the mother doesn't want the father to see the child anyway, the mother will have no concern for the importance of the scheduled weekend with the child's father and will not try to schedule even trivial events around the father's weekend. This could come after a demand for more money or an unmet request solicited by the mother.

In cases when there is a long period of time, like during the summer vacation, the mother will literally reserve some of the father's scheduled days for her own plans, further cutting into the allocated time for the father's visitation. This can happen week after week for years. The child on the other end may have become accustomed to not seeing the father, or even worse, think the father does not want to see them.

Whatever the reason, the intended result is that the father will become so frustrated that he'll give the mother what she has demanded, or just give up trying to see the child. The mother then can say what she's always wanted to say; that the father is not trying, or does not want to see their child.

Tactic 2
You Can't Reach Them When It's Time To Pick Up The Child.

The mother could make herself unavailable when it is time to pick up the child by not answering the phone or the door, or not being at the designated pick-up spot.

What Are the Man's Options If the Child Is Being Withheld?

One father told us that after several attempts to see his daughter, he went to the court system to let them know that the mother was not abiding by the visitation order for scheduled weekends. The court's response to him was to go to the police station with the visitation order to have the police physically remove the child from the home. Because the child was already extremely confused and emotional about her feelings for her father due to negative input from her mother, the father thought it would cause more harm to the child by bringing police to her mother's house to remove her. The child was young, and the father didn't know if the mother would get violent and retaliate. In this case, the father continued to pursue a relationship with his daughter. Year after year, visitation was withheld and eventually the rejection came from both mother and daughter. Years of father bashing by the mother, and the mother's plot to never let the daughter have a relationship with her father, left the father with feelings of hopelessness.

Should the father have taken her out of the house by police escort? People will have different takes on whether it was right or wrong. The fact is, it should have never gotten to the point where the parent had to choose between causing a possible life-scarring event, or seeking other ways of developing a relationship with his daughter.

Some fathers opt to keep records of every missed visitation and then request custody, using the recorded data as evidence. The key to getting real results is the competence and experience of your lawyer. If you enter the court room representing yourself, unless you are a lawyer by profession, you will see little positive results. A good lawyer, however, will show that you are very serious about seeing the child, and you may stand a greater chance of getting the visitation you desire.

The Decision to Deny Visitation Hurts More Than Just the Father

The decision from the mother to withhold the child doesn't just affect the father and child; it also affects the extended family, and others who love the child. For example, in a new marriage, the stepsibling may be an only child, which makes the relationship with their other brother or sister from their non-custodial parent important. The mother of the child denying visitation does not see the disappointment and hurt that comes when the two siblings can't be together. If she could look in the other household and see the crying, the questions and witness the consoling that has to take place when the child is not allowed to come over, it may make her respond differently. Who knows? Maybe not.

When someone is hurting, and vengeance and manipulation stems from hurt, it is difficult to see anything but one's own hurt. Wounded people rarely think their actions may effect more than their target. Their actions claim other causalities along the way as a result of their decisions.

The One-Two Punch: Being Denied Visitation Especially When You Are Paying Child Support!

I find it amazing that some women will not allow the parent be a part of the child's life, yet they have absolutely no problem receiving money for raising the child. In many cases, the mother makes a continued effort to receive the monies owed to her for the child, but will not put the same type of effort into assuring that the father sees the child.

In the process of researching for this book, some of our "good dad's" deepest hurts come from the humiliation of supporting a child that they are not able to know. These "good dads" act with integrity and pay child support even though they are denied contact with their children.

The court requires that you pay child support for your child even if you are not able to see them consistently. They don't have any provisions or make any type of adjustment to the amount owed should you be denied visitation, because the expense of providing housing, food and other needs remains.

Constant Raising of Child Support

"I'm going to get all the money I can get."

"I don't need to go to work, I can live off of the child support checks!"

While a child should have support from their fathers, some men find they are constantly being hit with increased payments without a genuine need for the increases. From the mother's viewpoint, the father may owe them for not being with them. Or, the intent of the mother may have always been to have a child with the person in order to secure their financial future.

When greed is the motive, the focus may not be on the needs of the child, but more on the fact that there is a court system that is partial to women that can be quite generous when approving a raise in child support. Some men are still required to pay large amounts even when the mother has more financial resources than the father.

Tainting the View of the Parent - Character Defamation

Defamation is defined as the malicious injury
done to the reputation or name of another.

When the mother talks badly about the father or deliberately tries to taint the father's image, she is actually defaming the child as well, because the child is a part of the father. The mother tainting the child's image does nothing but bring negative repercussions for the child as they try to define what role their father plays in their lives, and who they are as it relates to their relationship.

No parent should talk negatively about the other to the child
regardless of his or her opinion of the parent.

In an effort to sabotage the relationship, the custodial parent will often lie about the other parent to create a false image of the parent. The father and the picture you paint of him will be the meter by which your male child measures himself. If female, perhaps it will be the deciding factor in the husband they choose.

The Mother Tries to Replace the Child's Father with Her Boyfriend

"I have a boyfriend now, so he can be his father"

In cases where the mother of the child is without a man in their life and the father of her child is not present, it is understandable that they will want more input, discipline and the structure that comes from the presence of a male figure. However, choosing that you don't want the father to be that male presence when they have the desire to participate as a father, is wrong. When the mother takes on a boyfriend or husband, as a father figure, they sometimes can demean the need of the biological father. Ironically, if the same mother had no man in her life, she would be the very one demanding more parenting time from the father. When she no longer values the need of the father, she will use the new man in her life as the surrogate.

In stepparenting there is the presence of another person parenting the child. However, the stepparent is never a replacement for a father or mother. Parents have so much inside of them to deposit to their children that only they can provide. So while other male and female figures can serve important roles in the child's life, one should never think that the input of that child's parent is not critical or unneeded. God made it that way. The biggest mistake that can be made is putting the child in the uncomfortable position of feeling that someone has come to replace their father, and making them to believe that this is right. Children are done a great disservice when they aren't allowed to receive from their father what fathers were created to instill.

Verbal and/or Physical Abuse

In another case, one of our "good dads" talked about when he was going to pick up his son and was physically assaulted by the mother. He chose not to strike back. Instead he made record of what was done in an effort to make the mother realize she had to control her anger. When filing the report with the police officers, he was not taken seriously. Again in the face of outsiders and himself, he lost, because the mother could still continue her tirades without having to account for her actions. In the eyes of the court, the mother's actions were acceptable because she was a woman and mother. It makes us wonder if it had been the other way around, how fast the response or belief would have been?

Emotional Games Played with His Children

False Sense of Losing His Kids if He Disciplines

Some men have had so many conflicts and games played by the mother that when they do get to see their children, they're afraid that their kids will desert them when they are disciplined. As a result, non-custodial fathers let a lot of things go in terms of disciplining the child. Why? Because they don't know when they may see the children again! These fathers are so happy to finally see their children that they try to give them everything when they do visit to make up for all of the missed time. They don't want to give any reason to create conflict in their relationship with their child, so they overlook any bad behavior.

Many Have to Be Satisfied with Hit-or-Miss Relationships

Fathers can be placed in situations where the mother has so much control over the father's relationship with his child, that if they see their kids, it's when the mother and child choose. If the child and the father have not had time to bond, the child will have no allegiance to the father, and can mirror the mothers stance which may be one of manipulation. Often the father feels that no matter what he gives the child, the relationship is lacking.

If tainted by the mother, the child may treat the father as just someone who is there to provide them with money and things, caring little about developing a relationship. This usually occurs after years of the mother blocking visitation, talking bad about the father, and the father being seen as an absentee father. When the mother does allow communication between the child and their father, it can be because they want something. In this instance, the child will learn to value what the father can give them more than having a loving relationship with the father.

To the father, although they are happy to hear from their child, they will feel horribly used, especially when they really desire the relationship to be based on love and not "things". The child may visit when it's beneficial, and never really get to see that they are missing the opportunity to develop a relationship with their father.

The strongest of men can have their spirits crushed when they reach out to their children time and time again in hopes of developing a relationship, only to be made to feel like the child has no time for them, and really doesn't care to get to know them.

Being Negatively Stereotyped By the Court Systems and Environment. "You've Seen One, You've Seen Them All"

When dealing with the court system, some men found that they were treated like deadbeats even if they had legal representation. While dealing with your individual case, you may experience extremely long lines, be shuffled around, and given the run-around by the employees.

One of the fathers we interviewed stated that in a hearing with his child's mother, even when he and the mother agreed upon a price for child support to be reduced, the mediator stepped in and denied the request, simply stating that they didn't think the mother meant what she said about their agreed upon request. The judge, in turn, raised the amount.

The system can be partial to the mother, and fairness sometimes takes a back seat to gender. Most of the time, unless the mother is really proven to be heinous, or if the father has a great lawyer, the mother is favored in custody and in court.

Although there are tons of advocacy groups for mothers, the scale still seems to be unbalanced when it comes to fathers, their rights, and entitlement to fairness under the law.

A lot of men simply don't know what their rights are as it relates to their children. One of the best things a man can do is research their rights, get written information from the court, and seek professional legal help.

When Seeking Custody or Joint Custody May Become an Option

The father may not have counted on being a full-time parent or even having joint custody, but when faced with not being able to see their child, or concerns about the quality of the upbringing of their child; joint or full custody of the child may be considered. In situations where the mother is being unreasonable and not allowing the father to be a part of the child's life, the father may get so fed up that he wants to petition for more rights with his child.

Two things to consider are 1) your motives and 2) your capability to raise the child. Make sure that if you petition for custody, you are prepared to rearrange your life to be able to give your child what they need to flourish. Seek professional advice to help determine what your chances are for winning. Always consider the best interest of the child. Even though the mother may be wrong in their keeping the child from you, she still may be able to offer the child more than you will be able to, depending on your current circumstances.

Be aware that should you pursue custody, it may help the mother get over any ill feelings she may have towards you when she sees that you are serious about wanting to be a part of the child's life.

Adversely, a legal move can backfire. The animosity the mother harbors may increase, setting the stage for a major legal battle.

Some Tips On What The Father Can Do To Protect His Relationship With His Children

Persistence, Perseverance, & Humility

Persistence:
Some men stop seeing their children after being denied visitation over a period of time. Strive to be very deliberate about the choices you make, and make constant strides towards establishing your relationship with your children. Whatever it takes, keep the lines of communication open between you, your ex, and your children.

Perseverance:
After numerous attempts and even court battles, you may feel like giving up. Never quit without pulling from your reserved strength. There may be times when your child may not show much interest in having a relationship with you. Even then, pursue. Your method may change in terms of how you relate to them (through cards, trips, etc.), but try to demonstrate that you care. Be determined to develop a relationship with your child so they can see for themselves who you are. It may not be until they are grown with children of their own, that they realize how much you went through to be a part of their lives.

Humility:
Don't give up when the mother does everything she can to make you want to quit. The ex may bad mouth you, and the kids may lose interest, but be determined to humble yourself. Choose not to react without a cooling off time. Choose not to hold grudges. Be the bigger person. Continue to try to communicate with the other parent.

The Bottom Line, Keep Fighting, Your Child Needs You
We all look to our parents to know right from wrong, good from bad, and it is not until we reach some level of maturity that we are

able to make decisions apart from our parents' advice. Parents hold a great responsibility and a wonderful gift, the ability to shape a life. It is therefore our responsibility to be fair, put the needs of our child first, and despite our own prejudices, provide sound, truthful, and good moral examples to our children. With all that being said, we must put our feelings aside when it comes to our children's view of their parents. A child needs to feel like their father is strong and invincible. Fathers will have shortcomings, and may not always make the best decisions, however, it is not the other parent's job to share, or taint the child's view of their father. The respect and security that comes from having a father figure alone adds to the quality of the child's life, and will aide them in becoming strong men and women, and even parents.

Part Two

*Getting Married
With Children*

Chapter 7
Leaving It All Behind,
<u>*except*</u> *my children!*

What happens when one of the parents decides to get married?

If in fact a child is born through a relationship other than marriage, there are many different roads the new parents may choose to travel after their child is born.

They Could Actually Get Married

Creating a child together can cause the parents to feel that they need to "do the right thing" and get married. Years ago, it was completely expected that if you got a woman pregnant, the right thing to do was to "make an honest woman" of her and your child by getting married. Remarkably, those marriages actually had a better survival rate than marriages today. It seems that people valued the family institution more, doing everything they could to make it work and choose to stay married.

They Could Pursue a Serious Relationship Together, or "Live Together"

Some people don't want to actually get married, but they want to try the person out to see if they are marriage material. Instead of getting married, they pursue a mutated form of marriage which is cohabitation. For some, the route of living together, especially once a child is born, is their way of positioning themselves as a family unit. The parents actually assume the roles of husband

and wife, appearing and acting as if they are married, although they have not legally or religiously made the commitment. The unfortunate side to this arrangement is that very seldom will the parents actually get married. The emotional damage usually ends up being very severe because they have become so much a part of each other's lives. When they separate, the reality that they were not truly committed sets in, and the person who dissolves the relationship moves out and moves on. Realizing that you were only their boyfriend or girlfriend becomes a hard fact.

The Parents Vacillate Between Being In an On Again, Off Again Relationship

The mother and father go back and forth, in and out of a relationship. This can happen several times before the parents call it quits. What makes this relationship difficult to dissolve is that they have a child together, and are forced to constantly see each other. A child also has a way of generating hope of being a family, and getting married. The parents would do better to make a definite decision about their relationship, so that they do not further delay the progression of their lives, or add confusion to their children and loved ones.

The Parents Were Teenagers or Very Young When They Had Their Child

The parents may have been young when they conceived their child, with no plans of a future together. Over time and with maturity, they both learn how to parent and become more active in the child's life. The parents of some teenagers (especially in the case of young men with a promising future), will encourage the young men to not tie themselves down, so they can achieve the goal they had before a child was conceived. If this is the case, it is likely that the father will either become only a financial structure in the child's life or completely disappear; leaving the mother to raise the child alone.

The Parents Have a Strictly Physical Relationship

The parents may or may not have been in a serious relationship prior to conceiving the child. However, they no longer consider themselves in any type of relationship, and may both be seeing other people. Nevertheless, they occasionally have sexual relations with one another and feel justified because they share a child. This is the situation that usually causes the biggest drama when either person gets married. Although the parents were under the illusion that they are just sex partners, they didn't realize the tie they created through their convenient sex episodes. If the decision to stop sexual relations in order to move on is not mutual, it can get complicated. That is why clear lines have to be drawn in terms of the relationship limits, and neither party needs to cross back over the line.

The Biggest Truth Is:

Only a very small percentage of people who have children prior to marriage actually marry the father or mother of their child.

This means if the mother gets married, and has custody of her children, she will find herself being a package deal in her new relationship. Her husband will take on becoming both a mate and a father in their household.

If the father gets married, but only has visitation, he will come into the marriage with a child or children, and the new wife will have to share in the parenting process and responsibilities.

Everything Must Change, Only Your Relationship Your Child Stays the Same

When the parents are no longer in a relationship, and one of the parents makes an absolute decision to get married, the only connection between the biological parents at this point should be the concern of the child.

This could be a defining moment, one that signifies the end of any chance of a romantic relationship between the parents. Either parent may have secretly held out hope for a future marriage, primarily because of their child, and now is faced with a sobering fact that there will be no marriage.

It also is a time when the parent who is not getting married finds out that they may still have feelings for their ex. Although they aren't currently together, the parent left behind may have had hopes their ex would always keep them first on the priority list.

Some relationships between parents can go back and forth sexually and emotionally for months, even years. With marriage, the relationship with the ex has now come to a definite end.

Now it's official, one of you is getting married, and all bets of getting back together are off, and should be.

Some will handle the news with extreme retaliation – with the thoughts of "if you're not with me, then you will pay for it, one way or another".

Regardless of which parent it is, everyone knows it's a time of moving on with his or her lives. This should be a time where both parents develop their own plans for dealing with the transition, protecting and preserving what is most valuable - the relationship that they both have with their child.

A Conversation With The Parent Getting Married

For the parent that is getting married, you will need to realize that although you became a parent first, you have decided to commit through marriage your life to someone other than the biological parent of your child. You will have to figure out the delicate balance of bringing your child from a previous relationship into your new marriage without leaving your new spouse to feel like an outsider in their relationship with you. It will be important to carefully communicate with your ex that you are moving on to a committed relationship and starting a new life.

One of the things to remember here is that you will be moving from being single and having a relationship with your child, to being married and having a relationship with your child. You must be sure to never negate your role as a parent, but also realize that you are marrying someone who deserves to emotionally have all of you. This just means that the "you" that they are committing to includes a few other people! It will be necessary that you carefully examine the areas below:

Your New Spouse: Are They the Right Candidate for the Job?

When you have a child from a previous marriage or relationship, and you are choosing a mate, it will be up to you to preview and interview your possible spouse to find out if your child and your possible mate will be a fit. You need to make sure that your mate will be flexible and strong enough to handle what comes along with you, your child, and your child's parent. You are a parent, and you have to not only consider your happiness, but also take responsibility for being a parent to your child.

The 5 Questions Every Parent Should Ask As It Pertains To Their Children and Their New Spouse BEFORE Marriage

#1 - Do My Potential Spouse and I Have the Same Values On Child Rearing?

This is very important! As your child will be coming over and interacting with your spouse, as well as becoming a an integral part of your child's life, you need to understand that how he or she views raising a child does matter. You and your potential spouse will need to be on the same page here anyway should you decide to have children of your own. Communication is key, as well as taking every opportunity to have your child and your new spouse interact with each other to get to know each other prior to marriage.

#2 - Am I Ready to Let My Potential New Spouse Be Seen and Respected as an Authority figure in My House and with My Child(ren)?

Single parents find that they have a hard time allowing their new spouse to be seen as a parent to their child from a previous relationship. This is particularly true of women who have custody of their children and have been the main authority figure before they marry.

The truth is that you must be able to present and respect your new spouse as an authority figure, and show that you are in partnership in everything, including parenting. This in no way means that the spouse is replacing the other biological parent. At the same time there must be a level of trust that you have for your new mate when it comes to interacting with your children. That trust and respect must be demonstrated to your child's other parent as well, so that they understand that you are encouraging a relationship with your child and your new mate.

Unification is a crucial part of a blended family. For the new spouse, they have to accept that you have a child with someone else, and that is a hard pill to swallow, even for the most loving and mature adults. Simply put, it did not include them in one of the most special events in your life. To exclude your new mate in the parenting process sends a message to them that "You are not welcomed in this area of my life. This is me and my ex's child and you're just my wife (or husband), so keep your mouth closed". If you choose to take this route, your spouse will be very hurt by your actions and feel like an outsider. Until you can include your potential mate in your child's life, it would be better for you to think about whether or not you are ready to get married.

#3 - Do I agree with, and am I Comfortable with the Way My Potential Spouse Interacts with My Child? Are They Tolerable, or Caring?

Be aware of how your mate really feels about your child and if they are willing to work on cultivating a relationship with your son or daughter. Are they just going through the motions because they want to be with you? Or, is it because they love you, and want to be a part of your child's life? If they are faking their feelings, rest assured when the pressure is on, their true feelings will surface. You want to make sure that the person you marry will make a continual effort to care for your child and their feelings.

#4 - Am I Confident That My Potential Spouse Will Treat My Children as They Would Their Own?

Honestly observe their interactions to see if your potential new spouse treats your child differently or with less consideration than they would their own biological child.

While feelings run extremely deep for biological children, when you marry someone who has children, the potential spouse will have to realize they will be taking their spouse's child(ren) in as their own, without showing favoritism. This especially rings true when both parties have children or plan on having children together. Unfortunately, if the future spouse does not have children, you might not be able to recognize this until a baby arrives.

If your new spouse has children, make sure that you make an effort to get to see them interact in their family environment very often. But be aware, if your new spouse has bad relationships with their own children, you really need to examine their parenting skills and give them the opportunity to repair that relationship before you get married. A bad relationship with their biological children may be an indicator that they may have some bad experiences with your children as well.

#5 - Will My New Spouse Put Out Fires with My Child's Parent if There Are Conflicts? Or, Will They Fan the Flames and Say Burn Baby, Burn?

If the soon-to-be stepparent is a positive influence on the parent getting married, they can actually add to the value of the parent-child relationship by bringing out the best attributes in their partner. By providing guidance, support, and stability, it may enable their partner to be a better parent. This especially holds true when the fiancé may have been in an estranged relationship with the biological parent, which in turn has affected the relationship between them and their child. Ideally, they should be able to be a voice of reason rather than keep the drama going.

If your new spouse seems to excite or cause more confusion for you and your children, that is usually a red flag that trouble is sure to follow. At all cost, be certain that your new mate will not make having peace in your home impossible. Your mate should be secure enough in themselves to give input, but not try to control disputes between you and your ex. You also want to make sure that your new mate is not a negative influence on you pursuing relationship with your child. Some insecure spouses may want to control the relationship you have with your children. It may be their attempt to limit future interaction with your children for their own selfish motives. If your ex has a hard time allowing you visitation, you don't need your new spouse to sabotage your relationship with your children too. If your new spouse has a major problem with you having a relationship with your children in spite of your wishes, and you desire to have one, you need to really think about the decision you are making. Anyone who knows the importance of a child having both parents in their life should be sensitive of the parent-child relationship. Should your potential spouse show lack of judgment, or patience, you need to ask yourself what kind of parent they would really be to your child anyway?

When Dealing With Your Ex

Be a Legal Eagle!
Make sure to have your legal papers in order regarding custody, visitation and financial obligations, so that when your ex realizes you are getting married, their personal feelings will not interrupt the relationship you choose to have with your child. Hopefully,

you have already taken care of this. If not, you really need to make sure your paperwork is in order as soon as you enter in a serious relationship. This is usually the first area that comes under attack by a hurt ex because it is seen as a form of power and a negotiation tool for the parent with primary custody of the child.

Establish an Emotional Separation From Your Child's Parent

This would be the time when you want to definitely discontinue any actions that could give mixed signals to your child's parent. Make it clear that you no longer desire any kind of intimate or emotional relationship with them, other than how it relates to your children. This does not mean that you become a mean person or treat them negatively; it just says that you demonstrate that you are in a committed emotional and physical relationship. Remember you are separating from your child's parent, not your child.

Don't Expect Too Much, Too Soon

Take it one day at a time and try to work toward a platonic, harmonious relationship with your ex for your children's sakes. You will find that you may be able to compromise on issues, and other times you may have to agree to disagree, but try to find a workable solution. It may take a while for your new marriage to register with everyone involved, so don't expect too much cooperation in the early stages.

Your Children

Talk with your children about your new marriage and spouse to reassure and provide them emotional security during this time of adjustment. Often children feel afraid that their parent who is getting married will leave them completely and that they may be replaced by new children in their parent's life. Let them know that you getting married will not change their time with you or your commitment to them. Make sure to work to be a constant force in your child's life. Demonstrate your commitment to your children by being consistent in visitation and meeting their financial and emotional needs. This will demonstrate that you intend to include them in your new life, although you no longer have a relationship with their parent.

Your Family

In order to start this new chapter in your life, make sure that the people closest to you are working with you, instead of against you in your endeavors to solidify your relationship. This can sometimes be a little touchy depending on the relationship your ex has with your family.

If your ex is close to your family, from their view, the parent is their grandchild's mother, your ex, and probably a part of their family. When a new spouse enters the picture, they may express that they want to see you, your ex, and your children be one happy family. Your family may feel that your spouse has stopped all hopes of that happening and their loyalties will be torn between their allegiance to their own family member and the ex.

The appropriate response from your family should be to affirm the marriage and be respectful of your choice. After all, it is not their decision to make. You have decided to make an official and emotional commitment that your family should honor and support. By not acknowledging or accepting your marriage choice, the family can make the new spouse feel like an intruder.

When legitimate and meaningful relationships have formed between the ex and the soon-to-be married parent's family or individual family members, it is unfair to think that the family should discontinue their relationship with the ex, even though the other parent has chosen to get married.

A good example comes from my own family where I have an aunt who I love dearly that divorced from my uncle. My invaluable relationship was formed with my aunt when I was very young. As much as I wish she and my uncle would have stayed together, they didn't. Although their marriage didn't work out, my relationship with my aunt did not end. She still regards me as her niece, and has since remarried; yet I treat her new husband with the utmost respect and try to reassure him that there are no hard feelings. It would have been unfair for me to do anything else, and really unfair to my aunt for not sharing in her new marriage and happiness.

However, be careful not to allow your family to be tainted, influenced or manipulated by your ex and their views of the other parent's new spouse because of their own personal feelings.

Talking with your family about your new spouse, involving them and your children with your extended family, and representing a united front between you and your spouse will allow your family to see how serious you are about the decision you have made and that their grandchild is in capable hands.

A Conversation With The Parent Whose Child's Parent Is Getting Married

Dealing with the Emotional Separation: But What About Me? I Mean Us?

If you were once in a relationship with your child's parent and loved them, and your relationship didn't work out, it can be painful. The person who is left behind feels as though their life and family have been destroyed. They cannot understand why things couldn't work out, and why things had to turn out the way they did. You could have actually been the initiator of the break-up and wonder if you made a mistake. Depending on the time involved, it could seem like your ex's news of their new marriage appeared quick and without warning. In the past, boyfriends and girlfriends had come and gone, sometimes too many to recall. You may have thought this relationship would disappear just like many others, only this time it is different and permanent.

Quite often, the spouse who is getting married can seem cold and distant, and they may need to be, because this is something they feel they must do to commit to the transition of marrying someone other than you. Consider turning to your friends or a support group for comfort. Allow your natural feelings of disappointment, anger and hurt to have the time to heal.

Coping With and Fighting Off Feelings of Jealousy and Retaliation

Don't deliberately try to sabotage your ex's relationship or upset the other person to get revenge. It is not a time to seek an increase in child support payments out of fear or anger, make aggressive physical advances, or try to cause trouble between your ex and his new spouse. Believe it or not, one day it may be your turn to get married. You will be the wife or husband, and will want your new union to be treated with respect too.

Learn the true meaning of forgiveness and get on with your life. If you choose to harbor unforgiveness and bitterness, it will hinder your future. In the end, you only really hurt yourself and your child because you won't accept that your ex is moving on with their life. Learn to let go of the past and look forward to the future. Make every attempt to be sincere at all times and don't play games!

Be Willing to Close the Door

Now that you have come to grips with the fact that your child's parent is starting a new life, you must be able to focus on your child's future. In order to move on, firmly close the door on past relationships. This closing of doors makes room for new opportunities. Learn from the past, let go of your emotional strings, and be happy that your child's parent will be able to provide a stable environment when your child visits.

Keep your integrity, and never let them see you sweat! Overreacting shows that you are still emotionally attached to your ex, and you're still hurt.

For the Love of Your Child, Have Your Paperwork in Order

If you have a child support order, make sure it is in accurate. And that your visitation arrangements are solid.

Child First, Your Personal Feelings Last

When reacting to a situation dealing with your child's parent always ask these questions:

"How is this going to effect my child?"
"Am I thinking about me or them?"

Thinking about your child first, and not your personal feelings, will assure that both your child and their parent get a fair chance to have a relationship. Resolve that you and your ex will not put your child in the middle of your communications, concerns, or anger.

Adjusting the Child(ren)

Talk to your child about their other parent's new spouse making sure to find out their feelings about the new relationship. Many times, your child will look to you to determine how they feel about their parent's choice. If you respond negatively or appear damaged, the child will feel bad about the marriage and the new spouse.

Even if you are secretly enjoying the fleeting idea of your child not cooperating, realize that it will only affect the relationship negatively. Your child needs both of their parents.

It's not about you; it's about your child.

Assuring them that you will be all right with their parent's decision to have a relationship with someone else will allow them to form their own opinions. If you go out on a limb, despite what you may be feeling inside, and demonstrate maturity, you can create a climate where your child will have a healthy relationship with their soon-to-be stepparent and parent.

Learning to Deal with Another Parental Figure in Your Child's Life

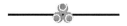

You're still their parent, but you will have to accept the fact that your child will have added parental influence - the stepparent.

Let's Establish a Few Things

It is natural to have feelings of jealousy and resentment towards your ex's new mate, because you may feel as if they are trespassing on personal territory – your child's life! Cool down. Take a breath. Remember, to put the child first. The happier the child, the better it should be for their overall growth and development. You want the other person in your child's life to be a positive influence. Keep that in mind as you encourage a loving and respectful relationship between them. If you are the custodial parent, you will have your child the majority of the time, so don't get intimidated or feel insecure when your child spends time with their future family.

What's Normal, What's Not in Terms of the Behavior of a Stepparent?

Although you desire the best outcome between your child and your child's future stepparent, be on the lookout for any signs that might indicate otherwise, but don't become paranoid. Communication is key with your child to determine if they are being treated well and are adjusting to their other parent's new relationship.

If you have any concerns about negative behavior of your ex and their potential mate, discuss it immediately. Allow them to handle or correct the situation, and give them the opportunity to address any concerns. If the concern is one of a serious or dangerous nature, you may have to contact the stepparent personally or the proper authorities.

It may seem like a bumpy and emotional road to travel, but if everyone acts with the child's best interests first, things will get better.

Chapter 8
Premarital Counseling 101

Marriage

Statistics show that more than 50 percent of all marriages will end in divorce. Why? Why do these couples get divorced? Could it be they were never really prepared for the journey? Did they have misconceptions of what marriage would be? Did they not understand that marriage is work, and it will be the effort that you put into the marriage that makes it worthwhile?

Marriage is more optional in the United States than it has ever been. Years ago, family formation rarely occurred outside of marriage. To a greater extent than ever before, one can choose whether to have children on one's own, in a cohabitating relationship, or in a marriage. Working-class Americans have radically separated the timing of childbearing and marriage with many young adults having children years before actually marrying. A significant portion of the increase in single-parent families reflects a rise in the number of cohabitating couples who have children, although these relationships often prove unstable.

One Year Preparing For the Wedding, Zero Time Preparing for the Marriage

When people do get married, they are ill-prepared for the actual marriage. Their biggest focus is the act of getting married; from picking the dress, to the wedding reception, and their honeymoon destination. When the love hangover has worn off and it doesn't work out exactly how they expected, divorce becomes an option.

Many divorces could have been avoided if the couple would have gone into the marriage with more communication, understanding, and clarity as to what both of them actually wanted and expected from each other. In fact, if people prepared more for the marriage before actually marrying someone, they may have found that they really weren't a match after all. The many misconceptions in troubled marriages could have actually been addressed from the beginning; with their counterparts being shown how to embrace their differences, and learn how to use both their strengths and weakness as stepping-stones in an effort to live as one.

Valuable and insightful premarital counseling and preparation can equip those seeking to get married with the tools they need to enter the marriage with realistic expectations.

Reginald Lane, Pastor of the Dunamis Outreach Ministries of Detroit once said it best.

> *"Ten years from now when you look at your mate whether negatively or positively, their happiness will be a direct reflection of how you treated them."* (Paraphrased)

Marriage Defined

One Flesh

The two shall become one. The union of marriage is just that - a union. Marriage is defined as the socially sanctioned union that reproduces the family. It is also defined as the legal union of a man and woman as husband and wife.

Two people come together and form one unit. They take vows and make a covenant with God and their spouse to go through the good and bad with this person, and always hope.

For this cause shall a man leave father and mother,
and shall cleave to his wife: and they twain shall be one flesh.
(Matthew 19:4-6 KJV)

Two Whole People Become One in Marriage

People mistake marriage for being the 'fix-all' for themselves; a solution to their relationship issues that will magically bring them happiness. The truth is marriage couldn't be any further from that idea. Marriage has a tendency to reveal what is truly on the inside of a person; quirks and feelings we may not even know exist. There is no relationship that cuts to the very depth of who we are more than that of a marital relationship. It is the relationship that leaves us the most vulnerable, exposing all of our ugliness. Our marital partners impact our lives so deeply, that it is imperative for both people to come to the marriage as complete and whole as possible. They need to be in a place in their own lives where they can offer nourishment to their spouse and their marriage. Nothing beats a supportive mate that can see your dreams and strengths, as well as your weaknesses and insecurities, and still be able to be your biggest supporter. Conversely, an insecure mate can tear one down to the very fiber of their being and create wounds that seem impossible to heal.

When you enter into a marriage with tons of emotional baggage (skewed ways of thinking, old hurts, feelings of inadequacy, and pains), those issues become the filter by which you view and deal with your life and personal relationships. People who want to have a long-lasting marriage should first 'clean' and rid themselves of as much personal baggage as possible so that they keep only that which is valuable and productive to their relationship.

Below are discussion points for you to explore, by yourself and with your potential mate. Make every effort to answer the questions transparently and honestly. Do not say what you think is right or what the other person may expect to hear. If you can't be honest here, then you will probably have problems addressing the issues should you get married. No matter how much in love you are, to enter marriage blind and unprepared is setting everyone that may be involved up for heartache and failure. Love them and yourselves enough to be objective. Should any conflict arise, don't over react; breathe, and look for solutions.

If it seems that the two of you are on completely different ends of the spectrum with no resolve, you may want to reconsider marriage. It is better to part ways now than to end up miserable and fractured later.

If the two of you seem like you can work together and go for the long haul, then by all means, start selecting those invitations!

Couples should remain transparent, embrace their differences which make them unique, and objectively analyze their family upbringing and relationship experiences.

Determine what you both share in common as it relates to your thoughts, and discuss what you would like to do differently in the future in your own marriage and with your family. This exercise needs to be a thorough self-examination of your life, relationships and dreams. Make it a candid discussion with your mate.

Is Premarital Counseling a Good Idea?

My answer would be YES! Marriage is a commitment that was designed to last a lifetime! Who starts any business, or goes on a trip without directions, and expects to get to their destination and have any measure of success? More time is spent on picking the honeymoon destination than on building the foundation for a successful happy marriage. According to Wedalert.com, most couples don't realize that skill-based premarital counseling can reduce the risk of divorce by up to thirty percent and lead to a significantly happier marriage. A good premarital counselor will help expose issues that may seem irrelevant now, but when coupled with the stresses of life, could turn into major problems for the couple.

Couples usually seek out premarital counseling with their religious advisor. The sessions can be as few as two meetings or as many as needed in order for the couple to work through any issues. When my husband and I got engaged, we went through nearly 6 months of counseling, and enjoyed every minute of it. While others may have seen it as just another item to check off of their wedding to-do lists, we found it to be an invaluable tool. It was there that we truly became even more transparent, and we always go back to the counseling as a reference for building a strong foundation.

During the counseling sessions, exploratory questions assess the couple's relationship. If you are afraid to expose and deal with possible flaws in your relationship before marriage, it could be your first red flag that trouble lies ahead. Discussing potential issues prior to your marriage could prevent huge blow-ups or even divorce later.

Are the Two of You Evenly Yoked; Will You Be On the Same Page?

One of the biggest factors in determining if your marriage will last is how evenly yoked you are on the issues. Evenly yoked means that you and your spouse are basically in agreement; share spiritual beliefs, your outlook on life, raising children, goals, money, etc. When two people don't share the same life philosophy; no matter how much they love each other, when decisions have to be made, they will find themselves heading in separate directions. No team can win if the players are pulling in opposite directions.

> *People can truly love each other, but not be going on the same paths in life. This is why you see people who look madly in love getting divorced everyday.*

What Is Your Idea of Love?

Everyone has his or her own definition of love. For some, love is when you just can't stand to be apart from the person. To others, love is how the other person treats them. To another, love is the butterflies they feel whenever they are with that person or hear their name. Before you marry and have a child, understand your future spouses expectations and definition of love. Women tend to think of love in emotional and physical terms, while for many men, it's a comfort zone. For them, the mere presence of another is love.

Love, However Is a Verb

Love is so much more than a feeling; it is an action word. Everyday the married couple will have to choose to love. Their love will become active as they demonstrate it by respecting each other, caring for the other, and considering the other's needs above their own. Long after the last guest has left the reception, and after the band has packed up, the couple will have to continually work on their love.

Although they both will grow and change with time, they will have to choose to embrace and respect each other's differences, encourage progression, and not be self-seeking, this is love.

But Here's Another Look into What Love Is:

Love is patient
Love is kind
It does not envy
It does not boast
It is not proud
It is not rude
It is not self-seeking
It is not easily angered
It keeps no record of wrongs
Love does not delight in evil but rejoices
*   with the truth*
It always protects
Always trusts
Always hopes
Always perseveres
Love never fails.

(1 Corinthians 13:4-8 New International Version)

What Is Your Idea of Marriage? What Marriages Have You Observed That You Like or Disliked? Why?

It is very important to examine these questions because we often base our likes and dislikes in marriage from family examples or from television (like Cliff and Claire Huxtable, from The Cosby Show, or All in the Family.)

The two people considering marriage should recall what they specifically liked and disliked about experiences filed under marriage that stick out in their memory. Was it that you hated the way that your Aunt Cheryl talked to your Uncle Michael in public as if he were an idiot, or perhaps the way your Grandmother always seemed to wait on your Grandfather hand and foot while your Grandfather treated her more like a maid than his wife. Whatever it may be, write it down and discuss the answers with your potential spouse.

In everyday married life, there will be some really high points where your marriage will inspire others. What many may not understand, is that you have to be faithful to work through the low points before swinging back around to the high points.

Marriage is a journey.

Marriage is what you make of it, and the best thing you can do is to make sure you are marrying the right person first. From there, be transparent and willing to do your very best to make it work.

Self Reflecting/Check Yourself

This section addresses looking at the man (or woman) in the mirror. Often times, when we desire to get married, we have already made up in our mind how we want the person to be: "I want him to be 6'2 with brown eyes, strong physique, love to work out, and love kids". We expect the person to be perfect for us. If this perfect person walked up to you right now, would you be their "perfect" person in your current state, or would you have some things going on that weren't attractive to them?

The premise here is to first look within yourself and take inventory of your pluses and negatives; your hurts and wounds. Work to deal with those issues and clean house of those things that would enable you to be the best "you" possible. Strive to be a good catch for your special person. If it means working on your temper, address it. If you have unresolved feelings about your father deserting you, seek counseling. If it's cleaning up your credit, get it done. And if you say you want a man that is in shape and you have been sitting on the couch with your friends Ben & Jerry, get moving!

Premarital Book Camp Questionnaire:

Some questions to ask yourself

- What do you need to work on before seriously considering marriage

- What are your insecurities?

- When do you feel most vulnerable?

- What makes you angry?

- How do you resolve conflict? Do you walk out, need some space, confront, act out, throw things?

- What makes you happy?

- How is happiness defined to you?

- Are you a jealous person?

- Do you have any trust issues?

- How important is affirmation to you?

-

Your Family Background

Our ideologies about life are derived from our relationships at home and the way in which we were raised. For this reason, looking at each other's family value systems and beliefs can reveal a lot about why a person acts the way that they do. Some people will embrace everything their family did as the gospel, and the way it is "supposed" to be done; while others can recognize things that they definitely would not duplicate in their own families. Discussing your individual upbringing will help the two people understand each other better and provide the platform for some soul searching that will need to be done before uniting in marriage.

Although it is quite natural to take on some elements of our upbringing, the most important thing to remember is that when two people get married, they are creating their own family. It is not a duplicate, it is an original.

Questions and Discussion Points

- How and where were you were raised?

- What was your childhood like?

- Was your family an affectionate one?

- How close are you with your family? Is that good or bad?

- What was your relationship with your mother? Discuss likes/dislikes.

- What was your relationship with your father? Discuss likes/dislikes.

- What were your parents' parenting style(s)? (i.e. strict, easy-going, you practically raised yourself

- What is the most valuable thing you learned from your mother/father?

- Is there anything that you definitely do not want to do that your parents did with you in your upbringing?

- How has your family treated people you dated before? Are they protective, embracing, non-trusting?

- Was there any abuse?

- Was your extended family an important part of your life?

Vision

Do you see your husband being capable of leading your household? Does the wife seem like she could raise children and still maintain a career, or will she crumble under the pressure of doing both?

Some people may not want to hear this, but the husband is the head of the household, period. This does not mean that the woman is being dragged by her hair, and is a baby-birthing machine, like in the Stone Age; it means that the husband should be the leader in the house. The wife is not walking behind him, but beside him; which means for the husband to lead he needs to know where he's going! The husband needs to have insight to see ahead, and plan for his family's future. It takes a certain level of maturity and vision to be able to anticipate the future of what you want your family to look like, identify the direction you already may be traveling in, and still be able to add to its progression. You can't do anything in life without first knowing what your goals are, how to do the task, and where you are going. With a marriage and a family it is no different. Although you may not know all the answers, being in a position where you have enough insight into going in the direction that appears to be right, is a necessity.

Family Goals Expectations (Yours and Theirs)

What are your expectations for your spouse and your marriage? What do you expect from your potential mate once you are married? Do you think that they should act differently now that you are official? Below are questions that will reveal how you expect your married life to be lived.

Children

Do You Want to Have Children? When? How many?

This question has to be answered honestly by both people. One person may be ready to have a baby immediately, while the other really isn't quite ready but goes along because of the other spouse. If not discussed, this may lead to resentment, which can cause a host of other problems. Now is the time to talk about it before you actually become parents.

You don't really want to find out after you are married that one spouse wants no (more) children after you are married. The decision when or to have children at all are one of the deal breakers, and can decide if you get married or not.

For example, say the two of you have decided that the mother is going to stay home for an allotted time after she has the baby. You have also decided that you would like to wait 3 years after you get married to start having children. Knowing this information can allow the two of you to budget for the mother being out of work for four months, enough time to cover the amount of revenue she would normally earn during the time she's at home with the baby.

Child Questions

- Are we going to have a child(ren)?

- How many?

- How long should we be married before having children?

- What's the plan after a baby is born? Will one of us stay home? For how long?

- How many years apart do we want to have our children?

- How will we make room in our lives for the child(ren) from a previous relationship?

What Is Your Parenting Philosophy?

Do you believe in spanking? How do you feel about respecting elders? At what age should our children begin dating? All of these are questions that may seem premature, but at least if you discuss them together you will get a better idea on what direction the person is coming from before the situations arise.

Goals – as a Family, Individually, and Careers

The purpose of these questions are for you to do Vision casting; a creative, strategy-based plan for your family. Vision casting enables you to create a visual picture of your plan for your lives together. Vision casting will assure that the two of you will be traveling on the same path, and will give the two of you a plan to pursue in reaching your goals for your family.

Goals Questions

- What type of house do we want? When will we own, and how?

- Where do we plan to live? In our hometown? In a hot or cold climate?

- How would you feel if we had to relocate for one of our jobs?

- Are vacations important to you? If so, how often?

- Is college/ higher education important to you?
-
- How are we going to divide up the household chores?

- Can we each pursue our own interests? What are they?

- Do you need or want time alone? Weekly? Daily?

- How will we make sure we have quality time together?

- Do you believe that we should be doing everything together?

Finances

One of the main causes of divorce is fighting over money. Before you marry anyone, you should be transparent about the debts and assets that you have. If you have debts, work to pay them off before you marry, or at least have a payment plan in place. Discussing budgeting, bill paying, and spending habits will also help the two of you take a realistic view of how you need to handle your finances to move forward.

Finance Questions

- Are you a saver or spender when it comes to money?

- Who is going to be responsible for making sure that bills are paid on time?

- How much do we owe in debts and what are our assets?

- Where will our money go?

- What are our financial goals?

- Do you have any outstanding fines or debts?

- What are our future plans for purchasing a home?

- What will be our 5-year financial goals? 10-year goals?

- What are your plans for our retirement? What age will we be? What will retirement life look like for us?

- College for our children, how will we save?

- How will we build our savings, and investment portfolio?

- Do you plan on staying in your current career, or do you have something else in mind?

- What would be your plan of action if you got laid off or fired from your job right now?

Sex and Intimacy

Depending on how you begin your relationship with your spouse, talking about sex may be easy or uncomfortable, but still has to be addressed. Candidly talking about your expectations and relating to them about your likes and dislike will be important to foster a healthy relationship. If either of you are completely new to sex, it will be important that you keep clear lines of communication and open dialogue about what you are feeling so that you can make sure that both of you are happy in your journey of intimacy.

Intimacy Questions

- Are you comfortable discussing your sexual likes and dislikes?

- What are your expectations of our sexual relationship?

- What is the frequency that you expect in our relationship?

20 Invaluable Tips for a Happy, Long Lasting, Healthy Marriage

#1 - Put your spouse first in your life before your parents, children, and friends

A good relationship consists of favoring your spouse over others, and is a delicate balance of not loosing your identity; yet at the same time, loosing one's self.

Self refers to the part of you that chooses to revolve 'only' around you, and is selfish in nature.

Before marriage, your priorities were ordered according to a single mindset. When you get married, your mate becomes your number one priority, second only to God. This does not mean that you become a cookie-cutter wife, or that you are "controlled" by another. Putting your spouse first simply means they should hold the top space in terms of what's important to you.

Sometimes the question is asked "What about children being put before the mate?" Relationships were designed to have a normal progression; two people love each other then get married. From their combined love comes the child. *(This is a little more complicated when the parent has a child first and later gets married. The parent's affection is towards the child, since there is no intimate relationship present.)*

When this person gets married, they have to establish their new positions with their mate and children, and come together to teach their child to respect the stepparent as an authority figure. (see more in Chapter 11 Stepparenting, Nuff Said)

#2 - You Will Have to Decide EVERYDAY to "Be In Love" Long After the Thrill of Being Married Wears Off

It's easy to love someone when everything is going right; they say and do all the right things, the finances are abundant, and you love the way they look. But what happens when the laugh you thought was so adorable now gets on your nerves? When you offer to work overtime because you don't want to come home to hear your wife nagging about the bills? When one of you gets laid off? And when what was once your "Brick House", now prefers to sit around and eat nothing but big meals?

The point is, everything evolves and changes. Yet it is our response to change that shapes our reality. Some days will be better than others. If you sincerely want to make it work, you will have to decide daily to love your mate. Long past the feeling, it is the act of doing things to show love. It is the way you care for your spouse and their needs, by listening to them and going out of your way to make them happy.

You get out of the relationship what you put in to the relationship.

As you give, have expectations that your actions will be reciprocated. But don't let your expectations be the only motivating factor behind why you are doing those things.

Hopefully, you will always feel the warm fuzzies when you think about your mate. Nevertheless, if you look up one day and feel fuzzy less, don't think the worst. It just means that you have to choose to love them, even though you don't have the just married 'glow'.

#3 - Why It Is So Important to Actually "Like" the Person You Marry

Couples that have been happily married for ten years or more have one thing in common; they actually like their spouse! Some may see love as an attraction, this overwhelming feeling that you can't be without someone. But to like someone past the romantic love really speaks to the longevity of your relationship. Now that person can actually become your best friend and your love.

When you actually 'like' your mate, everything you do is not wrapped up only in a typical romantic adventure. You can actually hang out together and enjoy each other's company. The more you enjoy being and doing things with each other, the greater your bond will be. Friends listen to each other, celebrate accomplishments, and relate to each other's dissatisfactions. We can talk and share with our friends, and we tell them everything.

As a matter of fact, one thing that holds true and signifies trouble in a marriage is when the couples don't want to share activities and interests. The ultimate sign of trouble is when they separate.

In marriage, friendship and respect are invaluable which makes having your mate as your best friend priceless.

#4 - Communication Is the Key – Verbal, and Non-Verbal

They say that 90 percent of what we say is not coming from our mouth. Even if we never say a word, we are forever speaking. That being true, how we act will tell people what we truly mean or feel.

For example, if the wife has had a busy month at work and asks the husband to take out the trash week after week to no avail, she eventually may get so frustrated that she will do it herself. To her, the message may be "he doesn't respect me", or "he isn't listening to me".

On the other hand, if the wife works extra late all week, the house is a wreck, there's no food in the kitchen, and no plans for dinner, to the husband that sends a message of "she doesn't care about if I eat or not", why should I care about taking out the trash?"

In reality, the wife may have simply had a big project that had a deadline, and planned to make it up to the husband on the weekend. Maybe the husband is so concerned with getting the kids out the door to school that he "unintentionally" forgets the trash, although in the back of his mind he could still be thinking about the fact that he has had takeout for the last 5 days!

Should situations arise where you are feeling hurt or disrespected, it is important to be able to share your feelings with your mate and not let the actions build up until they are on the brink of causing an explosion. Sometimes people actually have no clue their actions are affecting someone else.

If on the other hand you are trying to send a message, it would be better to address the issue openly to the person instead of dropping hints, hoping to get your point across.

#5 - What Caught Them Needs to Keep Keepin' Them!
While this may be a touchy subject to some, keeping your appearance up is important in your marriage.

We all age, and get older, that is inevitable, but you should want to always present your best self to your mate.

After all, you are a reflection of your mate. If you began the relationship wearing your best clothes, exercising, and leaving a sweet aroma that lingered in the room after you were gone, don't trade that in once you have them by becoming a couch potato and wearing last weeks clothes for the next two weeks. Remain the person your spouse wants to keep on their arm. Take pride in how you look to the best of your ability. It will not only make you feel good, but it will make them a little extra proud to be with you.

#6 - Try to Out Do the Other in Being Kind
Think of it as a race or a competition. Who can be more kind to the other? The couple that embraces this concept has the whole marriage thing in their pocket!

When you make it a habit to do something nice for someone and they are trying to do the same thing, you have no choice but to be happy.

If you start this out from the beginning of your marriage, it will help tremendously and can be fun too!

#7 - Respect Each Other

When you respect someone, you appreciate, honor, and revere them as a person. You are concerned about how they are treated. Do not confuse respect with fear. Fear takes the tone of doing something because you are afraid of what will happen if you don't. When you respect someone, you will consider how your actions will affect them, or if they would approve of your decisions. When there is a lack of respect, a person will demonstrate that they could care less as to how someone feels through their actions. The nail goes in the coffin when the person has been continually disrespected to the point that their confidence becomes destroyed.

> *When a person feels that you don't respect them,*
> *it gives way to a whole host of negative feelings*
> *that can cause a marriage to crumble.*

How to Act When Handling Conflict

#8 - Don't Feel the Need to "Have" to Be Right

Arguments and disagreements happen in every relationship. It is the way you respond to the disagreements that dictate their outcome. Often times people view an argument as their time to debate and win. In all actuality, if you win that means someone loses, and in a marriage you are one, so you both lose. While it is perfectly understandable to want to get your point across and heard, what it shouldn't be about is that things always have to be your way.

9 - Be Quick to Discuss and Settle Arguments

When disagreements happen, immediately talk with your spouse, and don't allow negative feelings to linger. The longer you hold something in, the more you will replay what happened, what was said, and begin branding in your mind the negative feelings associated with the actions. Soon the argument will take on a life of its own, and become much larger than it's beginning.

The only time you would delay immediately responding would be if you feel you will address the problem with anger or yelling. If this happens, give yourself a couple of minutes to cool down, and then discuss the issue.

#10 - Be Willing to Forgive

There will be instances when your feelings get hurt and you feel wronged by the actions of your mate. If this happens, be willing to forgive and move on. When you don't forgive and harbor hurt feelings, you start building a fortress whose fruits eventually turn into lack of trust. Usually, the person holding the unforgiveness is the most affected, and the person who has apologized bares none of the weight you are holding. Release them and yourself by truly moving past the problem, and don't revisit what you are forgiving.

Along with being forgiving, practice never going to bed mad.

Resolve any issues with your spouse before bedtime, and don't let strife carry on into the next day. Allow the new day to start fresh with 24 hours of opportunity to love each other, and life.

#11 - Be Slow to Speak, Quick to Listen, Be a Great Listener

Listening should be a part of what we do in all conversation; as to hear what someone is truly saying helps you understand him or her, and therefore can help you relate more effectively.

If you do get into an argument, listen to the other persons gripe. Allowing them to speak and get their thought out completely without interrupting, usually will give them time to vent and get their point across. The lack of extra adrenaline demonstrated by you will distinguish some of the anger. Listening will allow you to hear what they are saying, and respond based off of being able to hear their heart instead of reacting off of emotion.

#12 - Acknowledge Accomplishments and Things That Matter to Your Spouse, No Matter How Small They May Be to You

Become your mate's cheerleader, encourager, motivator, and supporter no matter if you think the accomplishment is great. If they think it's great, than so should you.

Even though we talk a lot about the two of you becoming one, each of you will have goals and attributes about yourself where you exist as an individual. Being supportive to your mate in the things that are important to them will go along way, and help them foster that same support to you.

#13 - Celebrate Occasions

Be respectful of and celebrate special occasions like birthdays, anniversaries, and holidays, and don't let it require having to be constantly hinted about for you to be reminded.

A lot of wives, in particular, complain that their spouses don't acknowledge what should be important to them both, like anniversaries. After all the hard work most of us do throughout the year, to get celebrated on these choice times, or even "just because", is not a lot to ask. Everyone wants to feel appreciated.

#14 - Eat Dinner at the Table Together: Talk, Be Refreshed, and Refueled

Whatever you do, make it a habit to eat at the dinner table with your family. Turn the television off, put down the phone, and focus on each other. Coming around the table was once an American ritual that became replaced with eating in cars, eating in front of the TV, or eating in separate rooms. Eating together as a family was supposed to be a therapeutic environment where there was a time of refreshing, fellowship, and communication. At the dinner table, parents could talk about their day, and children could share in what went on in school and learn table etiquette. Everyone could unwind. Sharing food with each other and talking is a way of bonding and adds security and stability in family relationships.

#15 - Plan Date Nights

The married couple should pick one night to go on a date. This will become increasingly difficult with children, but strive to maintain a day set aside for you and your mate to recharge your relationship. Find out what interests them and take turns doing things that the other would enjoy. While you may have your favorite places you frequent, also tryout new places to keep things fresh. This will keep your relationship exciting, and help to relax stress you may have encountered during the week.

#16 - Say I Love You Often

Saying "I love you" multiple times in a day; when you're getting off the phone, or maybe when your away, is a reminder to yourself and your mate that "Hey, I do love you". Remember your words have creative power; so continue to speak that you love your spouse often.

#17 - Watch the Company You Keep, If You Are No Longer Single, Don't Constantly Hang Out with Your Single Friends

Once you become married, you will have to adapt your lifestyle to your new marriage. Going to parties with single friends just doesn't gel the way it did before, because you are not single. Your single friends may be picking up the opposite sex and doing things that single people do. You, however, do not hold the same perspective because you are in a committed relationship. To keep placing yourself in that atmosphere would be asking for trouble. Be aware of what you allow yourself to be exposed to and your marriage.

Single friends are still friends; it's just that you might have to change how you spend your time together, and your conversations.

Find married couples you like to be around, and that share common interests. Being around other married couples when you are newly married will help provide good examples, resources, and great sounding boards for questions you come across in your marriage. The key here is finding couples that have sound advice.

#18 - It Is Your Marriage; Don't Let Your In-laws or Anyone Else Become Involved In What Happens in Your Household

Many marriages have been hindered as a result of meddling parents. When the two of you marry, you marry each other; your wife is not your momma, and your husband is not your dad. Therefore, leave them out of your marriage! Your parents had their opportunity to invest 18 years plus into raising you and providing direction. Now as an adult, they have to allow you to live your own life. As a married adult, constant involvement in your marriage from your parents could be crippling to your union. If this becomes an issue, it will be the responsibility of the spouse (whose parent's are getting involved) to make it clear to the parent that their involvement is not necessary. It shouldn't get to the point that the other mate has to say anything; because it would likely be taken negatively. Parents may not approve of decisions made by their children, but in the end, it is not their decision to monitor their son or daughter's household.

How a parent can assist with their child having a happy marriage while they are young:

- live the example of a good mate before their children

- demonstrate integrity

- instill values

- equip their child with good decision making abilities

- pray in advance for their children's mates; that they be someone deserving of their love.

If a parent has done their job in raising their children, they should be secure with the choices their children make, and not interfere.

#19 - Always Believe and Hope for the Best

Your words have creative power, what you speak, hope, and believe becomes your reality. If you say "they will never change", they probably won't, because you speak and believe they won't.

Believe and expect the best for your marriage and your mate, and watch the words you speak take action in shaping your relationship.

#20 - Finally, If You Want to Have a Happy Marriage, Be Transparent, Willing to Compromise, and Communicate

In today's world, it is a great feat to find someone to exclusively spend the rest of your life with in marriage. The greater challenge, long after the wedding and honeymoon, is staying married. The greatest challenge: being happily married, and raising happy, well-rounded children.

Take the time to make sure you both are ready and willing to commit to each other.

If so, put in the work before you say " I do" to make sure that your marriage will last a lifetime.

Chapter 9
Yes, I Will Marry You, All of You

"And the Two Shall Become One"...
But In This Case One with a Little Extra!

Years ago, when two people joined together in marriage, they entered the union with just themselves, and the only "blending" to speak took place with the extended families, and the couple's personalities. Believe it or not, a lot of couples were not living together either. Times have changed significantly, to say the least. Today, more couples who decide to marry will begin their relationship in some sort of blended family that involves children from a previous relationship.

Usually in a marriage ceremony the couple is admonished to leave their former lives behind and join with their mate to create a new life together. This, however, cannot be true as it relates to children that are a product of a prior relationship. It is now you, the person you decided to marry, and the result of their past relationships - their children and their parent- the ex.

This chapter examines what the spouse will need to be aware of prior to marriage to assure they are up for the challenge of living the blended lifestyle, and not enter blindly, or wearing rose-colored glasses. It is possible to achieve balance in both your new marriage and in your new blended family. People who get married with children have to look ahead to what they may encounter raising a blended family together, and develop a plan to help them deal with the situations that occur within their family.

Some Reality Checks For the Spouse to Understand When Getting Married to Someone Who Has Children

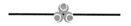

#1 - Realize You Will Be Starting Your New Life with Some of the Past

When you marry someone with children, instead of starting with a completely new slate, you will have to share your spouse's past through their existing children with someone else. A successful union can only occur when you are comfortable with their past and their child(ren).

#2 - Yes, I Will Marry You, ALL of You – Defined

One thing that cannot be denied: when you marry the love of your life, you also "marry" their children. Parenting starts here! Your paternal feelings that were reserved for a few years down the road have been called into active duty now that parenthood has been accelerated with your future stepchildren.

In addition to marrying their children, you will also inherit the children's mother, the mother's new spouse, and any other relatives that the ex has. The plain and simple fact: You inherit your ex's LIFE and all the baggage that comes with it!

When the child has its first basketball game, it will be you, your spouse, and your stepchild's bio family in attendance. When it's decision-making time, often your opinion will have to be voiced through your spouse. The list goes on and on, because raising a child is a commitment shared between parents. Your spouse just happens to be someone else's parent besides your children. To look at it any other way would be setting yourself and your mate up for failure.

Your Money Is <u>Their</u> Money

It is perhaps the hardest pill to swallow, but true. When two people wed, they may have past financial obligations, and maybe some property. These are all matters that can, with time, be paid off. Eventually they will be out of your life when the financial obligations have been met.

However, when you marry someone with children, their past is suddenly brought into your today and becomes part of your future. Your finances are no exception.

News flash!
The money that you and your spouse earn is not all yours.

Yes, you both earned it, but others will partake of the fruit of your labor. In essence, although you had nothing to do with the creation of this child or children, when you marry, even indirectly, you too, will be paying for the financial responsibilities of your mate. No court will base alimony or child support solely on the new spouse's income. However, from a cash flow standpoint, the money spent on your spouse's "other" family is money that cannot be saved or used to pay your own bills.

#3 A Parent Should Support *Their* Child

There are instances when the money the custodial parent receives will surpass "the needs" of the child, and is used for other things which could be anything from clothing for themselves or another child; bills, shopping, car notes, etc. As the spouse, can you deal with that? Some would rationalize that using money on bills and car notes, are justified by saying that the money for the other expenses are for the child to function.

#1 The fact is that a child's needs must be fulfilled.

#2 The fact is that two people had a child. Albeit taking the chance of living separately, both parents share the expenses of the child.

Having custody of a child and receiving child support should not be a reason for the custodial parent to not earn money to contribute to the provision of their child if they are physically able.

#4 Paying Child Support May Leave Your Household a Little Short!

What happens when your spouse's children receive more money than what your spouse contributes to the new household? There is a possibility that the children outside of your marriage may very well receive more financial support then your own children. Can you deal with that? How will you feel when hundreds of dollars automatically are taken from your spouse's paycheck and you are struggling to pay your families bills? It's a sobering thought. Will you be resentful? Will it change the way you feel about little Kelly coming to visit? How will that effect the money you spend on the child for holidays, birthdays or when they visit? How will you feel if you know the ex and your spouse's other children have expensive shoes when you are shopping at discount stores? This is your spouse's past being revisited and being imported into your today. Even though it had nothing to do with you, your spouse's decisions pre- "YOU", will still impact your home.

Helpful tip: When you earn substantial money, it may be a good idea to have an account of your own

If your spouse ever defaults and falls behind on their child support payments for any reason the money in a joint account can be taken by the court to pay those financial obligations. The court does not take the time to determine whether or not the funds are all due to your hard work. They take it ALL, whatever they need to bring the amount current. This will be true for any joint assets- cars, etc. Is that fair? No, but after all, you two are one, remember!

Having an Instant family.

I Love You, and I *Like* Your Kids

I have seen men and women who marry people with children, and in fact are really not on-board with the idea of having the children actively in their lives. They look at the child(ren) as something to "deal with", not really accepting what they will experience by becoming apart of the child's life. In their minds, the relationship with their new spouse overrides any feelings about the child. When they have to interact with the child, they develop methods of coping. Children should not be reduced to something to be dealt with! Don't think that the answer will be in distancing yourself from your spouse's children. Failing to put energy into being an active part of your spouse's child's life will not negate the obvious; your life definitely includes them, and their other parent.

The Responsibility of Raising Children Other Than Those You Birth

So what if your spouse had children when they were very young? Depending on their age when you get married, you could find yourself being a young stepparent.

For example, take the average woman who marries at age 25 and her husband is 28. If your spouse had a child when he was 18, at age 25, you will be married and have a 10 yr old stepchild! By the time you are 28, you'll be the stepparent of a teenager. Wild thought, isn't it!

A new marriage, in and of itself, takes a lot of effort, especially in its infancy. Beginning a new marriage with children will call for a lot of self-sacrifice, maturity, and patience.

I highly suggest that your relationship is rock solid before you get married, and that you have thoroughly set up a plan of action. Read this book cover-to-cover to help frame your perspective.

Another word of caution:
For an easier adjustment, the interaction with your
stepfamily should begin prior to the marriage.

Time Shared

I bet you thought I was talking about a beautiful resort in Florida, right? Wrong! Time shared, or visitation, may occur every other weekend, holidays, and half of the summer, depending on how the visitation order is structured. This means that if the children don't live with you full-time, they will be in your home every other weekend. Your entire family will have to plan around those weekends and adjust their routines to accommodate the visiting children.

If you have no other children, the weekend your stepchild visits shouldn't be the weekend that you say, "I'm not going to be at the house" or it's "their weekend". It will be very important that the child sees that their parent has a complete life with you. The child needs to understand that "this is my father and his wife, he loves her, and they are a team". They will learn and come to terms with this through observation. Therefore, there has to be shared time on that weekend, both family and personal. This is your child's time with their parent, and rightfully so.

I can remember visiting my father and how special that time was. I looked forward to it and expected to have special moments whether it was catching a movie or just being with him. Every child who does not live with both parents probably feels the same way.

Being an Instant Parent, Your New Role and Responsibility

So how much responsibility should you have as a stepparent? Your spouse should set the tone for a healthy relationship, so follow their lead.

If the non-custodial spouse is in a position where they are just developing and cultivating the relationship with their child when you are, you will be building the parental foundation together.

Your Spouse Will Set the Tone For Your Relationship with Their Children. How Does Your Spouse Measure?

"Encouraging Spouse"

The encouraging spouse gives free course for you as the stepparent to be involved in all aspects of their child's life. Sometimes the Encouraging Spouse feels that you will add balance to the relationship between them and their children. In fact, your positive influence can foster a stronger relationship between them. This will take love, maturity, and security from the new spouse to do this. When this happens, the encouraging spouse finds that they are a better parent with the support of the spouse.

"Reserved Spouse"

The reserved spouse still feels that although they may be in a relationship with you, the child is their sole responsibility and may limit your interaction with their child. The parent can be deemed "reserved" because they still consider the biological parent to be the sole influencer. In other words, their new spouse is "their mate", but they take the stance that it's not your responsibility to discipline their child. Again, if the parent getting married does not allow their new spouse to have some type of authority, it will not allow the child to respect the stepparent or your marriage.

The stepparent will have to also determine personally how much of themselves they are going to put into nurturing of the new relationship. Time has a way of maturing people and making situations better. When a parent has their first child, they are in a continual learning process. With time, they learn, grow, and the love for their children grows as well. When you are brought into a ready-made family, know that as the years pass, if you approach things in a positive way, your relationship with your new stepchildren will grow as well.

Factors to Consider with Your Spouse's Children

Age of the Children When You Meet Them

There is a great advantage to marrying someone with a very young child. The child is able to grow up with you as a part of their lives, and may not remember life without you. They don't have the chance to view you as someone who has disrupted their family. For a new spouse, it is a great advantage as well because you will feel as if they have grown up with you. Your love and attachment for them will grows as well.

When Children Are Older

If children are introduced to stepparents when they are over the age of 8, it may be more difficult for them to adjust to the idea of a stepparent. Also to be factored into the equation is how long their parents have been separated. When the children are introduced as teenagers, they not only have their own views of relationships, but their thoughts are coupled with hormonal and emotional changes occurring within them. Give them time and space to adjust and accept you as a part of their life.

Children May Feel Disloyal

Some children will be extremely loyal to the other parent. Although they want to be closer to you, they may feel reluctant to develop the relationship because they don't want to hurt or disappoint their parent. The custodial parent will control this by the feelings they convey about the ex getting married. If the parent acts really upset, or takes it further by expressing verbally their dislikes of the other parent, the natural response of the child will be to shut down towards their custodial parent when sharing that part of their life. The child does so because they don't want to upset or hurt their parent. The only response that the stepparent and parent can do is to give the child time to adjust, and assure them that no one is trying to take the place of their parent. Talking to them about their feelings, and assuring them that it is ok to like someone else, will put the child at ease and will allow the child to be free to like the stepparent. The main person holding the responsibility on mending the gap will be the custodial parent. Whether they are considering the welfare and happiness of the child or their own, they will determine if this actually carries out on a positive note.

Your Life Has to Be Flexible

Children change the rhythm of your life. The woman or man who imagined getting married, waiting a couple of years to have children, and having the time in between to enjoy their marriage may happen to marry Mr. or Mrs. Right, except they came with children! The scenario now changes drastically because you will automatically have children - stepchildren. The person has to be up for the challenge because they decided to marry someone knowing they had children. When they accepted their spouse, they chose to become a parent. Talk about flexibility, and you are just at the beginning!

From the start you have to commit to compromise. The difference between having a biological child and taking on your spouse's child is that you don't have the opportunity to grow with them from the beginning of their lives and there is a third party who is the authority figure in their lives. As a matter of fact, you may feel like an interruption because you INSTANTLY become a parent, and you have to catch up to whatever age they are!
When my stepson moved in with us at the age of 14, we had a 7-year-old son. I had to adjust my parental mind to think high school.

I realized very quickly that raising a teenage boy was completely different from a 2nd grader in elementary school- A LOT different! It was a huge learning curve, and I didn't have any time to prepare.

With *The Blended Family Survival Guide,* you will know that it could happen one day to you as well. I really believe God was holding me by the hand, showing and teaching me through His love. Do your homework now while you have the time to mentally prepare.

Emotional Availability

How much of yourself are you going to give? Are you going to think, "Oh, I only have to deal with them this weekend", or are you going to embrace your stepchildren and say "Yes I've married you and your children, and I am going to learn to love them, as I have naturally fallen in love with you."

Even, if you choose (which I hope you do), to love them whole-heartedly, you also have to come to grips with the fact that they may not choose to do the same with you. How do you deal with a child that is old enough to form an opinion, and may resent you, because you are not their parent? How do you get respect? Do you choose to say 'whatever', and allow it be hellish living or build a relationship? Or, do you repeatedly try to win their hearts? Realistically, happiness in this area impacts your relationship with your spouse and your entire life. Being able to accept that no matter what their response is to you, you are in it to win.

Some Feelings You May Encounter Emotionally: Natural Feelings of Jealousy and Insecurity

When you love someone, you want to share everything with them, and enjoy as many first experiences as possible. When a spouse comes into a marriage with children and the person they are marrying has no children, it is natural to feel badly because you were not able to give your mate their first child, nor will you both be looking at the experience with brand new eyes when you have your first child.

If you don't have children, the mother or father of your child shares a bond with your spouse that you don't yet have. If your spouse and the parent of their child were in a relationship where they may have been together longer than you and your spouse, they may think they know them better than you because they have more history. Even your spouse's family may be more welcoming of the child's mother, and it can be downright uncomfortable for you. The family may not know what to do when you come in the picture, because your mate has a child with someone else. Even though they are apart, they may see you as an invasion to their grandchild's family.

Your Own Family May Not Be Happy with Your Decision

Some families view marrying someone with children negatively. The families want their child to have a fresh start, and view children outside of a marriage as unwanted baggage. If you love the person and want to spend the rest of your life with them and their children, it is your decision. Hopefully your relationship with your spouse and their children will prove them wrong. Every person that comes into a marriage with children should not be looked upon as a negative addition to a family. It is true that marrying a person with children definitely requires more energy to cultivate your marriage, but does not mean you should never consider them. Just know what you signed up for!

Conflict May Be Inevitable, So Care For Your Emotional Stability

Depending on the ex's level of maturity and the type of person they are, you may be viewed as an instant intruder, an enemy to their family. With marriage, any hopes of reconciliation go out the window for the ex. Even if the ex does not want a relationship with the spouse whose getting married, there may be a feeling of resentment in knowing that person will be with someone else. How they deal with those natural feelings will determine if they take on the role of a Baby Mama or deal with their feelings, move on with life, and wish you well (which is a bit of a stretch for most)! They could make your life really difficult if they so choose.

Some Factors That Will determine Your Level of Conflict:

- How the relationship ended with the biological parents

- The length of time since they were in an intimate relationship

- The current state of the mother's happiness and life

- Left over feelings associated with their relationship

- How your mate handled the break up

- The financial commitment of your spouse to support the child on a regular basis

- The emotional relationship (or lack thereof) with his child

So, be prepared for the worst, so that when things are good, they're really good!

Double Your Pleasure, Double Your Fun: When There are Multiple Baby Mama's/Daddies

It is not uncommon for an individual to have multiple children and those children have different fathers and mothers. That means you could possibly find yourself having to not only work with more than one ex spouse but two or three. Aside from the children being confused, the new spouse (who may have multiple blended families), presents even more challenging situations. Different women, separate relationships and backgrounds, multiple support payments and visitation times = a longer period of adjustment. If the other parent is taking the route of the Baby's Mama or Daddy, you can have two people making your life difficult at the same time. You may be pulling double duty in the drama department.

When dealing with multiple mothers/or fathers, the rules are still the same with the exception of a few things:

- You may have to deal with multiple DRAMA!

- When you and your mate have children it will lead to a lot of explaining and potentially uncomfortable discussions about their siblings. The children will wonder why they have different parents, or why their parents aren't married.

- For example, one of the expected questions may be when your daughter asks her brother, "Why do I call Mommy," "Mommy" and you call her Sarah?" Or, "Why didn't you marry my mommy?"

- As a family unit, you may have no weekends to yourself due to visitation with the other children. If there are multiple stepchildren, it would be wise to schedule visitation on the same weekend so the children will get to know each other, and so that not every weekend will be taken up by visitation.

- Your financial obligation is multiplied ... many times.

- The spouse will have to get to know and nurture relationships with multiple children.

- Depending on the ages of the stepchildren, the new spouse will have to adapt to the temperaments and concessions of the different age groups and genders, which can affect the transitioning process.

- When one of the children is not able to come on their weekend, the other child may miss their sibling. You should want ALL of the children to know each other. So, with multiple children from different parents, it just makes building family relationships more difficult.

-

Being Understanding and UNSELFISH, Without LOSING YOURSELF

When you marry someone with children, you have to become unselfish, even if you wanted it to just be about you or your marriage, it's not anymore. If you don't look at it from that standpoint, then you're going to be pretty angry – ALL THE TIME, or at least every other weekend.

Yes, with every unrequested call, the occasional unannounced visit, and the sometimes blatant disrespect, you will have to always strive to be the bigger person.

The situation changes even more if you are the male marrying a woman with a child, because the chance is great that the woman has custody. That means you will become an instant live-in parent.

In a case when a father has custody of the child, usually bad circumstances with the mother had to occur for her not to have custody. If this is the case, by this time, the child really needs their father and intense nurturing from a mother figure. Not that you are ever trying to take the place of their bio mother, but it's that you are going to play the role of a mother.

Make Wise Decisions and Live with Them

Another reason for this book is that I want people to make wise decisions when they choose to have sexual relationships, or better yet, to abstain from having sex prior to marriage. People have to realize that EVERYTIME they have a sexual relationship with someone, they could bring another life into this world. Once they create the life, it is their responsibility to care for it. Regardless if it was a relationship or a one-night stand that turned into 18 years, the responsibility of raising the child remains. This book packages up for blended families what the journey will look like, and furthermore makes us all realize that parenting a child truly, is a lifetime job.

Believe that your marriage will be strong enough to be able to raise children, and at the same time, nurture your extended family.

So When You Go to the Altar. . . . . . .

And the minister tells you to repeat after him – it should go something like this ---um, hum, hum…

"*I, INSERT YOUR NAME HERE, take INSERT THEIR NAME HERE, -* and also little Cassandra, and Raymond, along with their parents, parents spouses', grandparents, and trials,

"To be my lawfully married wife/husband, - and also accept the ups and downs, commit MY finances, time, relationship, household, and emotions,

"For better or worse" – and it may get worse before it gets better,

"In sickness or in health" – your emotional health, that is,

"For richer or poorer "– that one speaks for itself,

"To honor and cherish" – your union, and their children,

"As long as we both shall live" – and definitely for the next 18 years plus,

"So help me God" (who is the only one who can help.)

"Yes, I will marry you, ALL of you."

If your answer is yes,
then NOW, and only now,
do I pronounce you man and wife
you may kiss your spouse
and embrace your life.

Chapter 10
What Did You Call Me?

How to Avoid Conflict and Take the High Road

Dealing With Conflict

Conflict: *an open clash between two opposing groups (or individuals)*

When dealing with the parents of a child in any blended family, some conflict is inevitable and should be expected. Situations will naturally arise when all of the parties attempt to raise their child in separate households while having to learn to relate and respect each other collaboratively. When you think about it, no matter how trivial or extreme, conflict always exists. Since the conflict is pertaining to mutually shared children, adults have to find ways to handle the discord.

Every person has their own mechanism for dealing with conflict. Some choose to instigate the initial conflict, some avoid the conflict at all costs, while others do a bit of both and choose to deal with it only when they absolutely must.

> *Conflict results in change, and change is something that some people have a difficult time embracing, especially when they feel that what they are presently doing is correct.*

The ultimate root of conflict happens when you perceive something or someone as a threat to some area of your well-being (physical, emotional, power, status, etc.). Threats typically trigger emotional or psychological responses which can lead the person to respond on the basis of their perceptions of the situation, rather than an objective review of it.

A person's perceptions (and reactions) are filtered through their:

- values
- culture
- beliefs
- information on the subject matter
- experiences
- gender

When conflict arises, these perceptions can make it appear that there are a limited number of solutions.

When the person's perspective is negatively influenced by their emotions, communication becomes difficult.

In the relationship between the parents and their spouses, a simple unresolved disagreement, may escalate into avoidance, verbal assaults, and resentment. In the worst cases, it may also lead to such an elevated form of hostility where the non-custodial parent may refuse to have any personal contact with their ex or their child. This is why it is important for the conflict to be resolved as soon as possible. If it goes unchecked, the child's well-being and their relationship with both of their parents will be affected most.

Knowing that there is discord is half the battle when it comes to conflict in your blended family and its counterparts. Understanding how to deal with the conflict is the other half. Being an effective communicator and peacemaker in your blended family will determine the amount of success you will experience.

It Is, After All, Only About the Child's Well-Being, Right?

By now you should realize that if there is no relationship between the unmarried parents, it's about the children, right? When dealing with conflict between the ex's and their spouses, the children should be the main focus when making decisions.

Often times if we were to step back and look at the conflict in the blended family, we would find that no matter how it is masked, the cause of the conflict is almost always centered around the adults, rather than the children. The reality is usually that one or both of the parents have not even taken the time to realize that their dispute is personal, not about the children.

It's All In How You Deal with the Conflict

As previously stated, there are plenty of opportunities for conflict. In situations when you're dealing with past relationships and feelings associated with a child and an ex, the emotion can be extremely intense with years of emotional layers. There are many factors, from feelings of resentment to disputes about money and visitation which become fuel in any conflict.

The question is, how you will deal with the conflict when it comes, and what role will you play in solving or eliminating it? Will you be the initiator or the person trying to squash it? Many times, we think to ourselves, "If I had just been able to think before I reacted, I would have handled the situation differently." At the height of anger, stress, or emotion associated with any conflict, our emotions became the major factor in our response.

People are constantly faced with making decisions about their interactions with spouses, children, and anyone they encounter. Let's take something that everyone can probably relate to - conflict on our jobs. In the work environment, we have to maintain a controlled frame of mind in our reactions or the results will be in disciplinary issues or dismissal. With our coworkers and bosses, we develop a tolerance level that allows us to refrain from completely losing control, dealing with matters differently than we may like. We know that if we really go off the deep end, there is too much at stake to lose. Any responsible adult, counts up the cost in situations that deal with their jobs to determine if the issues are serious enough to be willing to 'risk it all' to prove a point. For most, they are able to exercise a lot of restraint, because they understand the consequences. To avoid causing confusion or putting their jobs in jeopardy, amazingly enough, most people will bite their tongue, although they may be right. They think unselfishly; not about being right or wrong, but about sustaining their family.

The same concept applies to relationships when there are children from past relationships involved. It's not always about the adults. It's about the children, and that means that many times you will have to bite your tongue. Think about the repercussions of your actions and how those actions will affect others.

Do You Care What Image You are Portraying?

Another factor in people avoiding conflict on their jobs is their concern with the way their actions will affect the way people view them. They don't want to be viewed as irate or out of control by those whose opinions matter to them. When they are upset, they will choose another way of dealing with their feelings by either going somewhere private, calling a friend to talk with, or some other means of releasing what they feel. This type of self-control will be needed when handling conflict in blended family relationships.

You have to make a decision that every action counts and is being viewed by others. The difference between work and home is that the other adults, your family and especially your children, are the audience. In the work example, one of the main factors for a parent controlling their temper is the impact that losing their jobs would have on their children's quality of life. Likewise, when dealing with ex's, baby mama's, and spouses, it should be the same. In the end, it still should be about the ramifications in the eyes of your family and the effects on your child.

There comes a point when you will have to control your words and emotions for the sake of progress.

The Children Are Watching and Taking Notes

Another reason to master conflict is that you are the model your children will emulate when solving conflict in their own lives. If you do not get this area of your life under control, you will raise damaged children who will learn that when in conflict, this is how you handle it; "I do whatever I feel."

We have 18 years to really impact our children before they will be on their own. These lessons you teach while they are young will be the guides by which they make decisions and pattern themselves. Choose to make sound decisions and be a good role model for them to emulate when they are adults.

Honestly Identifying the Potential Conflicts

One of the most important ways to resolve conflict is by first knowing that the conflict really exists. The point in this chapter is to expose you to the potential conflicts before they happen.

For those who are already in some kind of blended entity, we will paint the picture so that you can see how your conflicts actually appear to others, and how to make different choices that avoid any conflict you may now be experiencing. When we know of the potential conflict, we can prepare ourselves mentally to avoid a reaction that may create an issue in the family. This is not to say that when conflict happens, you will automatically kick into resolution mode. It means that if you are aware and cognizant of your actions, you may take the time to think and react differently.

If you can do this no matter how much drama someone else creates, you will have reached a triumphant state of mind and a great level of maturity.

It will not always be easy to control your emotions or an automatic response. In fact, it is a moment-by-moment decision that you will have to learn to consciously make. You choose to make the decision to be mature and to think about your children's welfare always, period. It will also be a chance to show that you are moving forward in life and have left the past emotional connection with your ex. Believe it or not, when you get to that place, it will bring you a certain amount of peace.

What And Who Causes The Conflict?

Conflict Between The Two Biological Parents

Parenting In Two Different Households

In general, the mere fact that the parents are raising their child in different households, and thus, different worlds itself can cause conflict. Because the parents have different ways of doing things and have no intimate relationship which might make compromises easier, they have to always consciously decide to be flexible when either of them does something in child rearing that the other doesn't agree is correct.

Old Baggage

The feelings associated with the reasons the parents parted have a lot to do with how the parents relate and communicate with each other. The emotional baggage from their broken relationship becomes difficult to separate from the ex as a parent. In many cases, when the parents have limited interaction, they no longer have an accurate perception of their ex's character and life.

Child Support Issues

Another source of conflict between the parents has to do with money. The non-custodial parent can feel like the financial demands of child support has been unfairly divided. While the custodial parent may feel like the amount received is not enough (even worse if the non-custodial parent owes money).

Visitation Issues

When the non-custodial parent is not visiting their child or is inconsistent with visitation, it can become a trigger for conflict. On the other hand, if the custodial parent withholds visitation or makes it very difficult for the non-custodial parent to see their child, conflict may arise when that parent makes an effort to maintain or establish relationship with their child.

Outside Parties

Ex's, significant others, or extended family member's involvement in matters regarding the children can sometimes initiate conflict, or keep the confusion going.

A voice of reason can cause people to act more maturely;
negative involvement can make matters worse.

Conflict Initiated By The Ex Towards The Other Parent Who Is In A Relationship

Jealousy

The new spouse may become envious of the relationship with their mates child and/or the ex.

- • Insecurity could develop because of the length of time the parents were together before the new relationship. The new spouse may be uncomfortable with the depth of knowledge and familiarity the ex has with their spouse through the past relationship

- Jealousy is a natural reaction for an ex when they find out that the other parent is getting married or in a committed relationship. The ex may have unresolved feelings and may experience the "I wish it were me" syndrome.

- Even though they may not want an intimate relationship with the parent of their child, the ex may be jealous that the other parent got married before they did.

- The parent that is getting married has personally improved their lives and has achieved some measure of success or happiness. The thought from the ex may be "Why couldn't you have been this new and improved person when you were with me? I went through all the drama and the hard times, and now they reap the benefits."

- The ex may feel threatened by the new family unit being formed, understanding that the needs of the existing child will no longer be first in the parent's priority list for money, affection and attention.

- If the ex is single, with a lower income and has custody, they may fear that their child may be taken away from them now that the other parent is married and appears to be in a more stable environment.

Denial

The ex may not be able to accept the fact that the relationship between them and the other parent is over, and is in denial that the other parent has moved on with their lives. When the ex is in denial, their conflict will be centered on the new spouse until they realize that the new relationship is a personal choice of the other parent to move on with their life.

Their Children

- The way their child feels about the new marriage can cause the ex to initiate conflict.

- Insecurity may be displayed by the ex once the realization that someone else will have the ability to influence their child.

- The thought of "You spend less time with my child now that you're married."

The reality may be that the married parent has started a new life, and now just has to learn how to balance the addition of their new committed relationship.

Respect

- The ex may feel that the new spouse purposely flaunts the marriage which ends up provoking conflict

- Being disrespected as a parent by the non-custodial parent or new spouse

- The non-custodial parent or their spouse talks badly about the parent in front of their children.

Money

- The ex may have legitimate feelings about the way their child's parent acts towards them or their children, (i.e. "You are doing less (financially) for my child now that you have another family.")

- The ex may feel like "You owe me money, or I feel you are not paying enough", which will make them initiate conflict.

Selfishness

The ex who acts selfishly operates from the bottom line of caring about their own feelings and themselves more than their child, or anyone else. The ex's stance may be that "I am going to be spiteful and evil *just because*" with no incident needed.

Conflict From The New Spouse

Disrespect

- Being shown a lack of respect from their spouse's ex or their spouses children

- Dealing with Baby Mama(s)/Baby Daddy(s) drama. The spouse may find themselves exhausted by the constant confusion, so they themselves begin to respond negatively.

- Their spouse does not address issues related to the ex or children, may be slow to handle disputes, and allows disagreements with the other parent to linger far too long.

-

Children

- The spouse may not agree with how the ex is raising the child (their rules of discipline in the home).

- Visiting child's influence: Feelings about how the child coming into their home affects their own children and atmosphere of their home when visiting.

Money

- The newly married spouse may feel that there is too much money being spent on the child(ren) in child support. The money that is being taken from their budget causes them to not be able to meet their financial obligations for their own needs.

- Being faced with sudden or continual increases of child support that may seem unnecessary, and negatively affect their finances.

- Feeling as if "I am paying for their ex's lifestyle"

Denial

- The spouse may not have accepted the fact that the stepchildren are a permanent part of their relationship.

- The spouse may not have accepted the fact that their stepchild's parent will be in their lives by default.

Time

- The stepparent may selfishly not want their spouse to spend time with their child, or may want to mandate the time they spend together

- The stepparent may feel that their spouse may spend too much time with their child, thus short changing their relationship or new family which leads to resentment

Jealousy

- Envy of the relationship with child or ex

- Insecurity caused by the length of time the parents were together before the new relationship. They may be uncomfortable with the depth of knowledge and familiarity the ex has with their spouse through the past relationship

- Any suspected feelings or suspicion of remaining feelings from their spouse towards the ex or vice-versa

- The desire to have a child together with their spouse,

- *"They have a child with you and I don't."*

Anticipating Conflict

When Does the Conflict Occur?

- Pick up and drop off for the child's visitation

- Social events or unplanned public encounters between parents, spouses, and or children

- School functions

- Intentional encounters by either party knowing the ex will be at a location (i.e. their job, church, family event, etc.)

- Telephone conversations and when communicating

What Are Some of the Triggers for Conflict?

- Visitation – the lack of or refusal of visitation time

- New Relationship - new girlfriend, boyfriend

- Marriage

- A new baby

- Holidays
  - loneliness of ex who may not be in a relationship
  - fights about where the child should spend the holiday
  - extra money wanted by ex for presents above already allocated support fund
  - the Ex feeling like they should be attending family holidays and special events where they may not be invited

- *or simply, just because!*

General Tips For Responding To Conflict

Conflict Is Normal

Treat it as normal and expected. Conflict need not be life altering or taken personally. Conflict is simply a part of life. How you deal with it is a daily choice. Choose to not give it undue importance.

Be a Good Listener

Remain open to see the other person's point of view. If you dismiss the other person's views and immediately assign blame, you may miss any opportunity for compromise that could exist.

Don't Judge

Try not to judge the other person's state of emotion. Even if you don't understand, acknowledge the person's reaction as a significant indicator of the need to get their point across.

Don't Overact

Focus on the behavior, individual situation or problem without attacking the person involved either verbally or physically.

Sit, Wait, Think, and Act

If it is necessary to address an issue, take time to think first, before dealing with the conflict. Some may argue that you should immediately be prepared to fire back. When dealing with issues concerning children, discussing the problem when everyone can talk calmly is definitely a wise decision.

Keep Contact Short and Direct

If you keep contact limited and utilize a cordial or polite silence to avoid fights, you can often extinguish flames that are being directed your way. When discussing issues, try to get to the point tactfully, and don't allow time or opportunity for more unwarranted issues to present themselves.

Remain "In Control"

Take control of potentially conflicting situations. Managing them before you allow them to manage you.

Responding To Conflict By Role

For the Non-Custodial Parent Who Is Married

You Are the Communicator

Take the lead in dealing with your child's parent, and any conflicts that arise. Do not burden your spouse with the responsibility of communication with your ex.

Try to Stay Current with Monies

Use every means possible to stay current with your child support payments. However, there are situations that arise like pay cuts, layoffs, and recessions that can drastically affect your income. These cuts can affect every aspect of your life including your household expenses.

Here's where it gets touchy. If the father has a job loss or pay cut, with a family to raise in his home in addition to children from other relationships, it is impossible to relegate to second place the needs of the family you are living with, and pay much needed money out to your family outside of your marriage. That is the sad reality. It is hard to even think about budgeting for other than your basic survival needs when you are down to your last dollar. You still want to be as fair as possible, but someone has to come up short. If you find yourself in this position, the best thing you can do is talk to your child's parent. Follow up with the court to get a temporary reduction during the financial difficulty which will resume when you have secured another source of income. This is definitely not an excuse to get behind with payments. Realistically it happens. As with any other financial commitment you may have, you have to use any means to make it right. In the short term, if you make it up to them down the line, eventually they will see that you are responsible, but you may also be viewed as the bad guy during the financial hardship.

Even though you may be struggling financially, you do have a responsibility to ensure that all of your children have a home, food, and clothes. Not paying support can have immediate consequences on the welfare of your child.

Adhere to the Visitation Schedule

If something happens to interfere with your visitation schedule, inform the custodial parent well in advance for adjustments to be made. But keep all communication about the child.

If your child's parent is prone to drama, meet in a place where you will have control (or witnesses). Do not allow yourself to go into a potential ambush, and don't entice arguments.

Listen to What They Have to Say Before You Speak

Hear them out first. This way, they will feel as if they've gotten everything off their chest. At this point they'll be more open to listening to you, and then respond accordingly.

Think, Then Speak

Think about what you are going to say before you speak. Because you had a previous relationship with your child's parent, you should know which buttons not to push. That's why it's important to think about what you say, so that you don't offend that person.

Don't Participate in Any Yelling Matches

Choose to throw water on the flame, not gasoline. If they are yelling but you remain calm, they will be the only one yelling. They will calm down when they can't get a rise out of you. Conversely, sometimes people only get angrier when they can't draw you into the drama. If this is the case, it's better to calmly leave and tell them you will talk later.

The Spouse

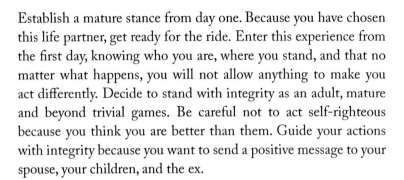

Establish a mature stance from day one. Because you have chosen this life partner, get ready for the ride. Enter this experience from the first day, knowing who you are, where you stand, and that no matter what happens, you will not allow anything to make you act differently. Decide to stand with integrity as an adult, mature and beyond trivial games. Be careful not to act self-righteous because you think you are better than them. Guide your actions with integrity because you want to send a positive message to your spouse, your children, and the ex.

At the beginning of your relationship you should not have issues with the ex. However, their reaction to you will be from a host of emotions that probably have nothing to do with you as a person. In fact, if you saw them on the street or at a place of business and did not know them, you would probably say hello, and maybe even strike up a conversation.

The way you handle the early stages of this relationship will determine whether things will end up smooth or bumpy, and in the end, cause you far more grief than you can ever imagine.

The key to making your life work is to know that your spouse's ex is just that, a past relationship. What adds another layer to their past relationship is their common denominator, a child. This child will connect all of you for years to come whether pleasant or not.

This Time is Different

Realize that even though you may have dealt with other baby mama's or baby daddies during your dating experiences, this relationship is different. You are now in a permanent marriage.

Rule of thumb is: Don't approach the baby's mama with negative expectations based on past experiences, or second hand opinions. Go in with a positive outlook. Let them show you who they are without jumping to conclusions.

Let Your Spouse Do the Talking

When it comes to the children and everything in between, your spouse should do all of the communicating. Calling the ex to voice your opinions or thoughts will only make things worse. After all, you really haven't lived their life, because your spouse had the relationship with them. When it pertains to the child, it ultimately is their place to talk to each other. This does not mean that you have nothing to say. It just means that in your household, you and your spouse talk privately about issues and problems. As time progresses, you may find that there may be more interaction between you and the ex once the idea of your marriage is no longer new, and there is a mutual respect.

If There Is a Problem with the Ex, Talk to Your Spouse

If you have been offended, or have concerns, talk to your spouse about it. Offenses and problems tend to increase and magnify the longer they are left unaddressed. Avoid voicing your concerns directly to the ex, but talk with your mate. Your mate should be open to hear your concerns, process them, and find a mature way to deal with them. The two of you will again have to be united in handling potential issues. Let your mate taking the lead in addressing the issues with his/her ex.

Communication with your mate is the key to avoiding the conflict.

When you do talk to your spouse, do so as calmly as possible. Plan what you are going to say and how you will say it. Talk it over with them to see if they agree that it is a legitimate offensive. Ask them how they plan to handle it.

Don't Look for Reasons, or Try to Find Fault

If you look, you will always be able to find reasons to dislike something or start an argument. If you view a person in a negative light, you just might bring about more negativity. Keep saying how much you dislike them and how awful they are, and you will probably get more bad behavior.

Your thoughts and words have power, so choose to want the best for the ex, and hope that they succeed in life so that they can be a good parent to their child.

That's Not My Name! Keep Your Cool

When your spouse's ex calls your home and goes on a tirade, don't respond to the madness! I would highly suggest that only your spouse communicates with the parent on the phone. This will alleviate a phone war. When there is a conflicting situation, think before you respond. You don't have to allow yourself to engage in an argument with them. It takes too much energy, time, and breath to argue. Strive to be a part of the solution, not fuel on the fire. At the same time, don't become a mat to be walked on or be verbally abused, know your limits.

When You Are Forced to Address the Conflict with the Spouse

No matter how much you try to avoid any conflict between them, sometimes by either running into the ex, them calling you on the phone, etc., you are put in the middle of the conflict anyway. Take the adult stance. Don't get into a shouting match or a physical altercation with the ex. Talk to them calmly, but be very confident. Instead, your stance should be to kill them with kindness. Having been caught off guard, they may feel embarrassed at their actions and may even back down.

On the other hand, they may feel like you are trying to patronize them or are being fake. In this instance, the ex may get even more upset because they want you to be as angry as them.

Remember to listen, make your point, listen again, look for resolution, and then regardless the outcome, move forward and move on.

Some Quick Tips For Spouses

Pick-Up, Drop Off

- If you are with your spouse when they pick up and/ or drop off their child, always be alert; be aware of your surroundings. While parked in the car, take off the seatbelt to be ready to respond to unsuspected actions where your presence would be necessary.

- Opt to not go if the relationship between the two parents is extremely estranged. Your presence can cause even more drama.

- If appropriate, be mature and wave through the car window at the ex. Again use common sense. If the act of you waving will incite a situation, avoid any physical acknowledgement. Occupy your time by reading, or chatting on the phone, but always be aware of what is happening outside the car. Look at something that will not directly have you staring at the exchange of the child which could be misconstrued as you having a problem with the other parent.

During Visitation

Rule of thumb: Do not do or say anything that you could not deal with if it were to be dished back to you. Watch your words and speak positively in front of your stepchildren. Also be aware of what you do because children in general are little human camcorders, recording your every move, action, and word in their memories.

Always Be Prepared to Expect the Unexpected

Remember to be flexible in your thinking. The person who was cordial, even nice on the phone, may have done a complete switch on you by the time you have to interact with them because of some unknown disagreement with your ex. Now that person has become the Wicked Witch of the East – all within an hour!

When You See Each Other

Be mature and speak even if you have to be first. If you don't get a response, move on. It doesn't mean you have to have a long conversation; it is just part of being cordial. Every situation is different, so exercise common sense.

Watch How You Share Your Experiences

They say there are six degrees of separation – which means the person you may be confiding in about how you dislike your spouse's ex, may actually know someone that knows them down the line. Again, watch your mouth, because your words have creative power. You don't want to perpetuate negative behavior by continually discussing it. If you don't want to hear what you say come back to you in another conversation, have a confidant. Do not talk to multiple people, because the likelihood that you may run into someone that knows your stepchild's parent is great. You may then have to eat some of your venting words!

Some Tips For the Ex

Make every effort to take the high road even though there are so many emotions involved; past hurts, jealousy, bitterness, fear, and stubbornness. Even the smallest of things can contribute to your reactions. After all, there was a whole life with the ex and your child before this new spouse came into the picture. Your anger and fear may not be because you want your ex, it may be the fear that your child will not get all they deserve because their other parent has a new life.

Even harder to take, is when your child and the new family seem to be so happy that you feel like an outsider. You don't see where you fit and you have the feeling that you, your love, and what you can give to your child, won't measure up to the whole package the other parent is providing.

Actually, you don't know the new spouse well enough to determine if you like or dislike them, your feelings are based on reasons other than them. It is the situation and the past that causes you, as well as your ex's spouse, to be at a crossroad where you will have to make tough choices. You will have to choose to either go forward with your head held up, or let your fears, emotions, and dislikes govern you. To accomplish this, you will have to think unselfishly, putting aside your feelings and putting the child's feelings first.

Ex Partners Won't Agree On Everything, and Old Emotional Baggage May Get Dragged Into Current Issues

Even though ex's disagree, because you love your child(ren), agree to work together respectfully for the good of the child. Focus on the matters at hand instead of old emotional issues by using effective communication skills. Working patiently toward mutual understanding can help diffuse potentially explosive situations.

Tips That Will Help You Build a Respectful Working Relationship with Your Child's Parent:

Take children out of the middle. Don't have the child relaying messages, spying on the other parent, or choosing sides. Try to communicate directly with your child's parent. If that is not possible, consider seeing a counselor or using a mediator to work out issues and agreements.

If your child is lucky enough to have the love and an active involvement of both parents (and, perhaps, his or her new spouse), that person will be a part of your life as long as you share your child. Raising children means a lifetime of sports games, dance recitals, school programs, graduations, weddings; the events and celebrations that add much to life's meaning. Your child will want to have both parents at those special occasions.

It does not make sense to be mean to your ex's spouse, especially when that spouse will be caring for your children when you are not present. If you purposely seek to manipulate, dominate, or intimidate in their collaborative relationship, you are provoking your ex's new spouse and causing them to associate negative feelings towards your child because of you. You're only hurting your child. If the spouse is mature, they will ignore your actions and try to treat the child as an extension of the person they married. However, if the new spouse is immature, you just may be setting your child up for unpleasant experiences.

The most important thing is that the child is getting to know their other parent and enjoying their time at their parent's house.

Avoiding Conflict Recap For Everupme

#1 - Watch Your Mouth, That Other Person Is Their Parent

No matter what your personal feelings are about the other parent, under no circumstance should you talk badly about the parent to your child. Regardless if you respect them or not, the fact still remains that they are the child's parent. The child should not hear negative things being said about their parent. Children are very smart and very sensitive. They can tell when something may not have been done right or said inappropriately. Actually, talking negatively about the other parent just might backfire on you as the child takes a loyalty towards the other parent, and gets upset with you.

For example, it is not appropriate for you to tell your child that the parent didn't pay child support. This doesn't achieve anything but hurt your child, in addition to building insecurity and hatred towards you for pointing it all out. It's not worth it. If you have a problem with the other parent talk to them about it. Do not talk about them to their child. Over time your child will eventually form their own opinion of who their parent is, and it's not up to you to define that for them. By all means, if the child is being lied to by your ex, or is in a detrimental situation, you may have to be a bit more frank with them, according to your child's age. Nevertheless, even in having heart to hearts with your children, try to not evoke pain and sadness. No matter what you personally feel about your ex, or their mate, in the end, your relationship is over, but their relationship is forever. Your child deserves it.

#2 - Mind Your Temper, Be a Lover Not a Fighter
Should you get to the point that you want to do bodily harm to someone, choose love instead of fighting; love for your children, love for yourself, and if you are the parent who is married, love for your spouse.

#3 - Practice Self-Control
No adult should have to resort to fighting with another individual to get their point across or to solve a problem. You could end up hurting yourself, someone else, or even find yourself in jail. If you have anger management issues, seek counseling to alleviate them. You will have to learn how to deal with situations other than physically. If you are approached with a physical threat, walk away if possible, or do what you can to get out of the area. After all, you have a child to raise, and being there for them warrants that you get yourself away from potentially harmful situations as quickly as possible.

#4 - Don't Do the Old Jekyll and Hyde Routine
Amazingly enough, nice people, when removed from their comfort zone, can find themselves doing a Jekyll and Hyde behavior pattern as a way of reacting to uncomfortable or hostile situations. Their actions can be irrational even to themselves. Their ex may bring out the worst in them. Old feelings, hurts, and memories may be on endless replay, which causes them to act the way they used to when they were with their ex. This holds especially true when the

relationship happened in one's earlier years. When this personality shift occurs, it is necessary to catch a realty check. Where are you are today with your life? Step back and realize that you are (or should be) a mature adult and your response should be just that. Don't allow your ex's attitude or demeanor to determine the way you respond or act. Things will go a lot smoother for everyone if each person is treated with respect.

#5 - Be Cordial

You don't have to invite them to a night out on the town, but try to be pleasant, or at least, as cordial as meeting someone for the first time. If they make every encounter uncomfortable, try to at least be civil and polite. You don't have to be overly involved in the encounter or the conversation.

#6 - Communication Is Critical

Communication is the vehicle to nurture and develop a child, especially when that child is being raised in different households. There will have to be communication between the parents and even with the spouses to raise a child. This means that you can't shut down and choose not to speak because you can't be heard or can't offer your opinion. When the biological parents end up in a place where they can't come to an agreement, the issue will not get resolved. The child will suffer the most, but the repercussions affect everyone.

For example, there might be a situation where the biological parents have a disagreement, and out of anger, one parent says, "Fine! I'm not coming to get him at all." There could also be a reversed situation where the mother is upset and suddenly an unmentioned sports practice or outing comes up during the other parent's visitation weekend. Now the child can't come over. Who loses most? The child who is stuck in the middle of two upset parents.

It will be very important to be able to talk (on the phone, text, or email), about the child's progress in school, special achievements, disciplinary issues, etc. In essence, catch up with the child's life. Regardless how you may feel, you have to put those feelings aside and choose to effectively communicate with your child's parent.

So What Happens When You Can't Communicate?

If you find yourself unable to talk, keep the other parent informed via email, voicemails, or by letter. Should disputes come that you can't resolve, enlist the help of a mediator either by the court, mutual unbiased friend, or religious counselor.

Don't Act Out In Front of the Children

Children learn more about acceptable behavior and interactions from what you do and how you do it, than by what you tell them. Watch how you physically respond when communicating with the child's other parent or stepparent.

This is why it becomes very important to hold conversations away from your children. Your children should not be placed in the middle of any argument, or hear anything confrontational towards the other parent. This rule goes across the board regardless if the child is living in two separate homes or not.

Children are like sponges at every age and are influenced by our behavior. If they are young children, they will think that the way we relate to one another is the example to be followed.

R-e-s-p-e-c-t

Respect each other, yourselves, and your child (ren).

Even if you don't respect the parent, pretend you do in front of your children. As they grow, they will be able to see what their parent is truly made of, and the parent may change for the better!

My mother and father divorced when I was very young, and they both knew each other's flaws. My mother, who raised me by herself, had every opportunity to say derogatory things about my father. However, her stance was always that he was my father and she wanted me to respect him.

My mother knew who he was positively and negatively. She knew that as I grew up, I would see for myself and draw my own conclusions. She never wanted to paint the picture for me. As an adult and a mother, I respect her so much for that. I experienced both disappointments and elated moments of joy while with my father. As I grew to be a woman, I came to understand exactly who he was as well as understand his strengths and weaknesses.

Could he have done more? Yes. However, I was still able to look at him as a father with the proper respect, and draw all I could from our relationship. He was still seen as a positive influence on my life.

If something disturbing happened that my mother didn't approve of while I was away for the weekend with my father, she would discuss it with my father. He would listen, and then they would both adjust.

As a young girl, I needed to feel like my father was an invincible man, even if not. Likewise, my father only conveyed positive experiences to me when he talked about my mother. My father knew it would shape how I saw her. Even more important, he also did so out of respect for her.In households where both parents live together, there are times when one or both parents fall short of the parental standards. In most cases, the parents are not as quick to talk badly about the other parent because they wouldn't like the effect it would have, or how it would change the child's impression of the parent. They try their best to live harmoniously in their home. Although the blended family is a different situation, the same idea holds true. All parties should respect each other, and the way they communicate their feelings about each other.

Conflict Resolution

Focusing on each person's vested interests (the children), rather than perceived problems, is a more effective way of handling conflict. Operating from this approach creates an environment in which everyone's needs can be expressed. Shifting focus to what's really important between the separated parents (the children), works to reduce the emotional drive to protect one's own emotional interests. The interaction between the parents and their spouses then becomes a solution-based exchange where the children are the main benefactors.

Chapter 11
Stepparrenting, Nuff Said

A Conversation with the New Couple: Let's Face it, Stepparenting and Stepfamilies Are Challenging

Join the Party, You are Not in This Boat Alone

Contrary to popular belief, all stepmothers aren't wicked, and all stepdads aren't hard-drinking, abusive men as they are sometimes portrayed. However, all blended families are not living in "blended bliss" like the *Brady Bunch* either! But one thing is for sure; there are a lot of us! In fact, according to the most recent statistics, one in three Americans is now a stepparent, a stepchild, a stepsibling, or some other member of a stepfamily. And more than half of all Americans today have been, are now, or eventually will be in one or more stepfamily relationships during their lives.

While parenting itself is a hard job, stepparenting is much more difficult. Stepfamilies are a result of the dissolution of a family or relationship where one or both parents at some point enter a new marriage. Parents need to understand that their children may still be recuperating from the emotional losses that come with a separation, and are in the process of accepting the physical changes in their family environment. Being new to the dissolved family, the stepparent will have to use strategies many people learn in their daily lives to build good relationships and become a successful stepparent.

When it comes to children and their acceptance of the new stepfamily, there can be a host of different stances the child may decide to take.

- You may be faced with young children who fantasize that their stepfamily will be just like their first family and may have expectations that are hard to fulfill.

- Conversely, you may have to deal with older children who have extreme loyalties to their other parent, and want to have nothing to do with forming a new family.

Regardless of the situation, it is the duty of the parents to redefine 'family' for their children and develop a relationship based on love and mutual respect.

Jupiter and Mars: Navigating Your Life with Child(ren) Living in Two Houses

Your children will be faced with living in two different household environments. The terms of your custody order will dictate how much time they spend with each parent. A great deal of mothers are awarded primary custody of their children; with the father being awarded visitation.

If awarded joint custody, they will spend their time at both parent's homes. Your children will have two physical homes, and literally, two separate lives. There can potentially be distinct groups of friends, siblings, extended family, as well as life events. Compounding the issues, there will be either new spouses or significant others.

Adjusting the child to the way a particular household runs can sometimes be challenging; especially if you are the one who does not have primary or joint custody. It means that the child is always in a state of adapting until both homes are stable enough to offer a consistency for the child.

It can also become a challenge when the two home environments are drastically different. For instance, in one home the parent could be single, and have a "structure-less, care-free" lifestyle, and in the other home, the other parent has a more family oriented lifestyle.

You can see where it can become extremely confusing for the child because although the parent may be comfortable with their own lifestyle, the child who is establishing their ethics could easily get mixed messages. And believe me, they are watching.

Your Biggest Asset: Unity

The keys to successful parenting in a stepfamily is the harmony in the marriage, and respect, both given and received. There will be two types of relationships that are at work in a family with stepchildren: the marital relationship of the couple and the stepparent-stepchildren relationship. Both will have to be nurtured and performed with extreme care to ensure happiness for all. How the stepparent and children handle the relationships in the stepfamily will determine the level of stress on children which in turn determines stress in the marriage.

It is a misconception that the stepparent alone is responsible for stepparenting. Both parents have to understand that it is not the sole responsibility of any one person, and teamwork is the name of the game. The strength of your love and affection for each other and your commitment to your marriage, will determine whether your relationship can endure the pressures and challenges of having a stepfamily while providing stability for your new blended family. There must be parental positions established for both the biological parent and stepparent based on their individual strengths, just as it would be in any traditional family. The parents need to have the same goals for their children and work as a team to achieve their mission – a well adjusted, happy, and secure family. The biological parent will need to balance their support of both their spouse and children as they struggle to adjust to one another.

Keeping Strength and Love in Your Marriage

According to the American Academy of Pediatrics, more than a third of children who enter into a stepfamily will later experience a breakup of that family. To save the kids from suffering through yet another divorce or breakup, it's essential to work on strengthening your marriage.

After all, you wouldn't be in a position to have a stepfamily if two things were not present:

> #1) Two people came together and pledged their love to each other, to share the rest of their lives together.

> #2) A child or children from another relationship exists that deserves love too.

Love is the common factor in both cases.

Although life can be overwhelming, especially when there are children involved, the married couple will have to take their time to keep romance and love in their marriage. Plan date nights weekly or on off weekends from the stepchild's visitation. Go to a concert, movie, or weekend get-a-way, just the two of you. Reignite the spark that made you fall in love.

You can't continue to pour out love without getting fueled back up.
Make time for love.

Establish a United Front to Prevent a Divided Union
Spouse with the Child Has to Take the Lead

Smart stepparenting means that the biological parent and the stepparent form an alliance to parent the child(ren) together when in their household. It is imperative that you and your spouse be on one accord when it comes to relating with the children, the children's other parent, your extended family and friends, discipline, and home life. When the couple presents themselves as a unit, it discourages discord or speaking badly about another parent. It is of great importance that the child be secure in knowing that their stepparent will treat them fairly and will be someone they can trust. If the stepparent is not sincere in wanting things to work within the stepfamily, their influences on the biological parent could be quite manipulative, and cause more chaos than peace.

The Parents Must Declare Their Support For Their New Mate to Their Ex

When the spouse relates to his/her ex, the relationship as husband and wife should be clearly established to the ex and revered to confirm the union and unity. In some cases, this will not be necessary as the other parent may be mature enough to be respectful of the union. This does not mean that the stepparent is trying to take the place of the biological parent. However, it does send a message of, "I respect my spouse as the male or female head of this house, we are one, I am committed to them, and the only relationship between the two of us is as parents of our child whom we both love." This position will give the new spouse a feeling of security, confidence, and strength which will make the journey have hopefully more ups than downs.

In the beginning, it is paramount that the union be formalized to the ex, to set boundaries and prevent misunderstandings that may cause division in your marriage and family. It will be very important that the spouse with the children take the lead in establishing these boundaries. If the stepparent tries to establish authority without the support of their spouse, it will only lead to headaches and unproductive results.

Experience Brings Empathy; At Least It Should

People who are products of blended families usually adjust better to having stepchildren because they have the personal experience of being in their stepchildren's shoes. Whether good or bad, experience was their teacher.

When the stepparent has experienced blended family living via divorce, or a past relationship, the hope is that they become more sympathetic to the stepchild and ex, because they were once in the same place. They can identify with the mixed feelings of inadequacy and jealousy when being a part of a family unit, and when spending time with their extended family.

I experienced this growing up with a single parent, and being a product of divorce. My parents were divorced when I was very young, but had a mutual respect for each other. During their marriage, and even after my parents divorced, my mother was always an advocate, encouraging the relationship between my father and my half brother. She was happy when both my brother and I would visit my father at the same time allowing our relationships to grow. My mother knew that because both my brother and I were our mother's only children, it would be important for us to develop our own relationship. I try to refer to my mother's example of security, maturity, and unselfishness as a model for how I interact with my stepchildren. To this day, she is still so very kind to my brother. She is ecstatic to see him and his family, and loves to see us interact. My mother is also a wonderful grandmother to my stepchildren. My father remarried twice, which gave me two sets of stepsiblings and we unfortunately never developed any kind of relationship. When I married and gained two stepchildren, from different mothers, I already had years of first-hand experience with blended families. The only side I had not been on was the baby's mama. Even with that, I learned a great deal from my friends who are in some of the same situations.

I know that my own hands-on experience in "living blended", made me sensitive to issues of stepfamily life, and gave me a different perspective on what the stepchild could be feeling. I remember both the good and bad of my experiences, and am thankful to have had both so that I could relate to my very own stepfamily.

A Conversation with the New Stepparent

Introducing the Instant Parent, I Mean Stepparent!

Ingredients:

1 Spouse who is a parent

1 Spouse with no children

Directions:

Add:

Children

Pour in:

Strength - Patience

Time - Communication

And Understanding

Blend Slowly. . . .

You said, "I will marry you; all of you." Congratulations! You are officially a new stepparent! You married the love of your life and want everything to be fabulous. You accept the fact that your mate has children, and enter into the union with a positive attitude and objective: to make them fall in love with you and you them, just as you have fallen in love with their parent. Welcome to the journey of self-discovery, parenting, and being an overcomer!

Being a stepparent is a very demanding role; you are now a parent, but how much of one? It can be confusing, especially if you have no prior experience with children. You will be parenting someone else's children and sometimes doing it with much resistance. In addition, one of the biggest hurdles may be the hidden fear you may harbor as you try to squeeze yourself into a position that you have never filled before.

Maybe you went into the marriage saying that you were fine with your spouse having children, but in all actuality, you have chosen to just tolerate the situation.

Be realistic with yourself from the beginning about how you plan to thrive as a stepparent. If you don't plan to actively work during the growth of your new family, you might want to consider getting married to someone who has no children. If you do nothing to cultivate the relationship, or make matters worse by being negative, you are setting yourself and everyone else up to suffer a slow death. After all, it's not just you affected in this stepfamily relationship. You have the child(ren), and your mate's feelings to consider.

Undoubtedly this will be a lot of work. It is time to separate common misconceptions from the reality of stepparenting. Half of the misfortunes come from never taking a true look at stepparenting or having a winning game plan. When you don't have realistic knowledge of what to expect, you may think you are experiencing something out of the norm, when in fact you are actually just working through the process that comes along with the task.

Most importantly, know that you have agreed to say yes to your marriage, and yes to this new life - including all that comes with it. Do all that you can to make it work.

If you come with children, know that your parenting style may have to adjust when dealing with your spouse's children because you are their stepparent.

Fear Is Normal In This Case

Allow yourself to have feelings of fear, envy, anger, and a sense of feeling overwhelmed. Those are natural feelings. It's what you do to overcome those negative feelings that will lead to a positive outcome and a stronger family. Don't allow negative feelings to paralyze your progress. Accept it, but don't linger in it.

Understand That the Age of the Children Plays a Factor

As stated previously in this chapter, your stepchild's age when you become a part of their lives, has a lot to do with their ability to adjust to you as their stepparent. Young children are easier to mold than older children who are more opinionated, and may have more baggage.

The stepparent may, in fact, take on a greater role in their stepchild's life, as in cases where the other parent is not present in the child's life at all. In any case, the child should be allowed to grow into the new relationship without having the pressures of the stepparent becoming an instant authority figure.

When I met my stepchildren, they were very young, so they basically grew up with me in their lives. They were both male, very courteous, and accepting of me from the start. It was not in my relationships with them, but the adults involved that required the most adjustment.

However, the story differs when the children are at an age where they are more aware, say at 9 years old, or one step further, teenagers. When you talk about teenagers, you have their life circumstances, hormones, and perhaps past relationships of their parents that they have to contend with, so it could be a little more difficult. The biological parent should take the lead when it comes to disciplining older children, particularly if it's a fairly new marriage.

Gender Matters

Boys tend to be more accepting of a stepmom than a young girl. The stepmother-stepdaughter combination is the most difficult relationship that results from two families joining households. Sometimes in a stepmother/stepdaughter relationship the young girl feels like "You are not my mother, I'm my father's princess, and you won't replace me." The same goes with two males as in the stepfather/stepson relationship. If the son has been the only male figure in the home, he may have subconsciously taken the role of being the "man of the house". When another man comes onto the scene assuming that role, there will be strife. If the stepdad is sensitive to the situation, he can provide a stability the boy has never had if a father was never present. This is especially true with the mom who remarries or gets married for the first time and has custody of her children.

Being a Part-Time Stepparent vs. an In-Home Stepparent

There are pros and cons dealing with the visitation time of the child(ren) for the non-custodial parent and stepparent in a new marriage (because the child(ren) will only be visiting every other weekend).

In most cases, the majority of the married couple's time will be spent cultivating their new relationship. However, they will spend valuable time with their child(ren) on visitation weekends.

In this scenario, the stepfamily has a limited amount of time to bond and adjust. If the road is a bit rocky during the transition stage, the couple gets to separate from the child(ren) for another week, regroup, reflect, and build strategies on how to make it better the next time they see the child(ren).

When the stepparent has the child(ren) living with them full time, the entire step-parenting experience is much more intense. On one hand, there is so much time to work on the relationship that the transition may be a little easier as the stepparent immediately takes the parental role. The stepparent now has the opportunity to learn through trial and error under the same roof. The only downside to this scenario is there's no time to regroup because you're in the trenches daily.

Expectations

Expecting instant attachment or love from your stepchildren may be an unrealistic ideal.

However:

- You have a right to be treated with respect.

- Set an example for them by treating them with respect, love, and kindness.

- Realize that they have a parent whom they live with the majority of the time, and that you really have a brief window of opportunity to build a relationship with each visit.

- Try to enjoy the time, and don't expect that this brief encounter will cause immediate change.

- With continued positive interaction, you can build a relationship with your stepchild and bring permanent influence over your stepchild's life.

Many stepparents don't immediately bond with their stepchildren nor have those 'parental' feelings. In fact, some stepparents go into their relationships with negative expectations, and come out pleasantly surprised when they receive acceptance they never bargained for. Embrace the positive energy, no matter how unexpected. Feed it and allow it to grow into a fulfilling relationship.

Give Yourself and Them Time

You have assumed a new role and like anything else, it will take time for you to learn and feel comfortable in your new stepparent shoes. It is not automatic. Everyone's adjustment time will be different. All parent's and children need time for their relationships to evolve.

For example, imagine starting a new fitness routine to get in shape or lose a significant amount of weight. After the first days of working out, it would be unreasonable to think you will have reached your goal and will fit into a new suit three sizes smaller. No, it will take training, discipline, action and consistency, to get the results you want!

Some Reality Checks – Lets Get Real!

Reality Check #1: Your Life as You Know It Will Change
The dynamics change for a stepparent once you get married. Now you and your mate are officially a couple, live together, and are working towards creating a home. You now have a more responsible role as an authority figure, and the child that you just happened to see occasionally now has a permanent schedule that causes you to interact with them on a consistent bases. Both you and the child will have to adapt to the changes and make adjustments to move forward on the road of discovery.

Reality Check #2: Loyalty to the Parents May Bring Guilt
Your stepchild may have such a strong loyalty to their parent that it prevents them to get close to you. You and your spouse will have to teach them that accepting you does not mean they are denying their biological parent.

Reality Check #3: You May Feel Like an Outsider
There may be times when you feel left out when your mate and their children are together. To combat feelings of being emotionally isolated, give your spouse and their child there own time, but also make sure to reserve time for all of you to do things together as a family unit.

Reality Check #4: You May Feel a Pressure to Step Up

You may feel like you are being forced to take over the role of the parent who is not present. If you feel this happening, talk with your spouse about your feelings, and set your own parameters.

If the parent is deceased, or not actively participating in the child's life, you may really need to increase your involvement as the missing parental figure. Sometimes you may be the only mother or father that child may ever know, and will be just as critical in their development as their biological parent.

Reality Check #5: You Are an Influence, Good or Bad

Understand that you will be an influence in the child's life - good or bad. Your relationship with them will affect the way they shape life and other relationships they encounter in adulthood. They should be able to look back and feel grateful for the knowledge and love that you added to their growth, and not be scarred for life or have bad memories of being mistreated.

Reality Check #6: Don't Try to Take Control

You can be an influence, but don't try to control the relationship between your spouse and their children; after all it is their child.

Reality Check #7: Drama Alert! Your Spouse's Ex May Try to Block Progress

Know that your spouse's ex may try to be a negative influence in the growth of your stepfamily due to fear of being left out, replaced, or loved less by their child. Until they are secure, he or she just may put a monkey wrench in as you try to progress in the building of your relationship.

Reality Check #8: Play the Waiting Game

Stepparents should not overact when stepchildren don't readily accept their parenting efforts. The parent of the child must still be the parental focus and the stepparent should still be grandfathered into parenting the child.

Foolish Assumptions

"We Will All Be One Happy Family, Right Now!"

Everything takes time. Just as biological parents have to cultivate and nourish their relationship with their child, so will you. It takes nine months for a baby to form and brought to a point where it can function outside a mother's body. How in the world do you think you are going to make everything be peachy keen in a couple of days? It's not going to happen. If it seems too good to be true, just wait for the other shoe to drop! Don't expect for everything to run smoothly from day one. If it does, that is great. Keep in mind that there are cycles in every relationship, and you have to give the new relationship time to develop.

"Everything Will Be Normal"

Normal is relative, especially when you are referring to blending a family.

Accept the fact that:

- Having children outside your marriage will be a challenge.

- Somebody else has had children with your spouse before you did.

- Your spouse is somebody's ex.

- Things will happen that will be beyond your control.

- You can't control other's behaviors.

- You can not allow disrespect.

I think the mistake most people face in finding their place as a stepparent is trying to make everything right. Then there are those who decide not to care at all about having a healthy, solid relationship.

A marriage consists of the journey of two people becoming one unit. Anytime the rhythm of that equation is disrupted, things are not going to be normal. I personally had to come to grips with the fact that no matter how perfect or idealistic I tried to make the relationships and happenings with my new stepchildren and their parents, there were going to be things happening that would be out of my control. The only thing I could control was the way I reacted to situations when they appeared. When I resolved that it was not a perfect situation and that there were going to be things that "happened", I could deal much better, and had more peace.

No More Drama!

Newsf Fash: Drama Is Sometimes the Inevitable

When people are not content with their own situation, they have a hard time finding happiness for someone else. It can sometimes be their mission to cause as much trouble as possible, and they don't mind using their child as a player in their games.

In the beginning of the marriage, it is very important that the stepparent allow their spouse to make the ultimate decisions when dealing with their child. When disputes arise between the two biological parents, defer the drama to them, and try to steer away. (more can be found on this topic in *Chapter 10 "What Did You Call Me?" How to Avoid Conflict*). As time progresses, there may be more influence from the stepparent when that drama directly affects the new family unit, as in a long-term problem with the child, or custody.

"I'll Never Let Them Get to Me!"

Don't think that negative dealings with your spouse's baby's mama(s) won't affect your marriage or how you view your mate.

When people have been in a relationship, they know just how to push each other's buttons. Your spouse's ex may do things that upset your mate, and bring out a side of your mate that you don't like or have never seen. The ex knows what will bring confusion into your home, and may want you to see what they consider to be "who they really are."

Remember that you are trying to move forward with a new life. The result of their past together is their child, but the future contains a positive direction for your family. Do what's necessary to maintain peace in your home and relationship. Remain clear on what you want for your marriage.

Strategies for Stepparents: How to Make It Work

Know Your Boundaries, Defining Your Role as Stepparent

Make sure that you and your spouse have a detailed discussion about what you both expect in this new family relationship. You need to first sit down with your mate and have a heart-to-heart about their children, what they expect from you, and what you expect from them as a parent and as your spouse. Discuss your spouse's expectations regarding your involvement in disciplining, guiding, and interacting with the child(ren). Don't be afraid to discuss your differences, opinions on parenting, and how you view solutions to any existing issues. Most importantly, be honest. If you don't start out being open in your communication, you will have a hard road ahead of you. It is my belief that the biological parent must take the lead in carving out the boundaries between their children and new mate.

Support, Your Biggest Role

The biggest role you will find as a stepparent will be that of supporting your spouse in raising his or her kids.

What do I mean by support?

Support is defined as:

- the act of bearing the weight of or strengthening

- giving moral or psychological support, aid, or courage to back, be behind, and approve of

- confirm: establish or strengthen, as with new evidence or facts

- corroborate: support with authority or make more certain or confirm

- be a supporting structure that holds up or provides a foundation

Showing your support to your mate in their parental role will be what they need from you to assist them in parenting their child and to further the relationship with both you and your stepchild(ren). Because your mate was their parent before they were your spouse, it will be imperative that you begin by assisting with the growth of their child, while allowing for your relationship to flourish as well. It will be a delicate balance, but if you enter this role in a honest, loving way, it can grow into one of the most rewarding relationships that you will ever have!

With time the stepparent may be able to assume more authority with their stepchildren. However, the adult/child respect level should be present from the introduction of the relationship.
Be careful to remember your position, don't overstep it, and do not take it lightly. You can only go as far as you are allowed to in your stepchildren's lives. So don't push, let it flow.

Woo-sah! Stay calm

When conflicting situations arise, and they may, remain calm. Don't be alarmed if your stepchild directs anger, jealousy and/or competitiveness towards you. Now that you are aware it may come, prepare for it, and try to keep your cool. If you respond and blow up in reaction to your stepchild's attacks, he or she ultimately wins. When they are angry, they may want to believe that you are against them. Instead, you and your spouse should work out a plan of action in anticipation of any conflict. In the event that conflict occurs, you and your spouse will both be on one accord in terms of the response.

Develop and Maintain Open Lines of Communication

Developing excellent communication in your new stepfamily will be one of the biggest assets you can have in getting to know your new family.

There may be a few things working against you in opening the lines of communication; for example, resentment from the child and the newness of adjusting to a person who now seems to want to be their parent. These negative feelings may not be one- sided. The new parent may also have their own feelings of inadequacy in being someone's parent.

In cases where the child is very receptive to the new parent, they quickly thrust emotion, actions and attention toward the new parent. When this happens, the new parent may not yet know how to reciprocate. It is an emotional give and take. If your stepchild immediately gravitates emotion toward you, even if you are not accustomed to reciprocating, make an honest attempt because they obviously want to bond with you.

Suggestions to Help Your Family Get to Know Each Other

#1- Learn How to Look for Nonverbal Expressions

Nonverbal communication is information communicated without words. About 93 percent of our communication is nonverbal, with

55 percent being displayed through facial expressions, posture, or gestures and 38 percent through tone of voice.

What this means, is that you will have to become a student of this unspoken language, paying close attention to what is being communicated by your stepchild, as well as yourself nonverbally. Non-verbals can include: posture, facial expressions, appearance, voice, tone, eye expression, smile, how close you stand to others, how you listen, confidence, your breathing, the way you move, the way you stand, the way you touch them, and silence.

If it means that you literally have to look at yourself in the mirror after you relate with your stepchildren, or ask a friend to observe how you act, do so. A great deal of what you give off to them and what they are saying to you, will be unspoken.

Take the time to shut down and listen. Be accepting of a child's feelings and give time for adjusting. When you listen to someone, whether they are talking audibly or non-verbal, it gives you the opportunity to understand their feelings, thereby identifying why they do what they do.

#2 - Take Time Out to Share In the Little Things

Take the opportunity to create special moments where you and your stepchild can have time to yourselves to learn about each other. This doesn't mean you have to plan a long getaway where you look into each other's eyes and have numerous 'heart-to-heart' conversations, so don't get tense. It could be as simple as watching their favorite television show, and then discussing it with them. Maybe you casually start a conversation about something you are doing and how they may be able to help.

My stepson really likes computers, so any time he would see me working on my website, his eyes would light up in curiosity to learn more. That is a special moment when we are able to connect, and where we relate. If you look closely, you will find or create moments of your own.

#3 - Take the Time to Find Positive Things in Your Stepchild and Then Tell Them

Look for the positive in your stepchild and talk about it with them. Give encouragement, show praise, but make it legitimate. When people know you appreciate them, it helps them to let down some of their guards.

#4 - Work to Build Trust

Every relationship relies on trust, and with a stepfamily you have to build that trust from scratch. By being supportive of your stepchildren, and spending quality time with them, you will send the message that you want to be apart of your stepchild's life. Most of all, follow through on what you say you will do, and make good on your promises.

#5 - Set the Tone for Positive Results and Visits

Have a positive attitude when anticipating your time with your stepchildren; it will take you along way. Expect that you will have good visits with your stepchildren.

- Make plans for exciting, meaningful visits that will make an impact.

- Realize that if your stepchildren don't live with you, every opportunity you get with them has to be a concentrated, meaningful effort.

- Try to impact their lives in the amount of time you do have, and make it count!

#6 - Prepare Your Home and Yourself for When Your Stepchild Comes to Visit

- Realize that this is the only time they see their parent. Allow them to have personal time with their parent, as well as shared family time where everyone joins in.

- Make them feel welcomed.

- Prepare the house with things they may enjoy, like their favorite foods, or go out to their favorite restaurant.

- Have a room or place made just for them; maybe a blanket that is used just for their visits, something that makes them feel a part of the house.

How to Handle Conflict

Discipline & Living in Two Houses, with Two Sets of Rules

When your stepchildren do not live with you, it is inevitable that issues about the way a child is raised and disciplined will arise. Maybe one parent is more lenient, and the other parent is very systematic. This becomes especially true when it is the custodial parent that is objecting to the means of disciplining. When these conversations come up, your spouse should take the lead in communicating with the ex, and then bring you up to speed on the situation. Then the two of you can come to an understanding about how discipline will be conducted in your home. Don't worry about confusing the children. They are very smart and understand the differences in parenting styles, just as they would if their parents were living together. You and your spouse will need to talk about consequences for actions and define the involvement that you will have.

When it comes down to discipline, this is another great reason that the two people entering a union must trust and know each other extensively. When you truly know the person you are marrying, they will make decisions with you in mind as to how you would react or want them to react, and will do what is in the best interest of the child, even when it is unpopular.

Dealing with the Infamous Four Words, "You're Not My Mother/Father!"

As a stepparent, your role is not to replace the other parent. Let's be very clear on that! Nor are you to become a friend to the child. It may be necessary to have a discussion with your stepchild and let them know that you are not trying in any way to take the place of their mother or father. Let them know you are there for them, and you realize that this is a change that will take time to adjust.

At the same time, there are rules in every home. When the child visits, they are not just visiting their parent's house, they're visiting your home. With it being your home, respect is an established requirement that must be enforced. That means even though you are not their bioparent, you are an adult and they will have to respect you, as well as the rules you and your mate have established. This takes a mix of firmness in a non-threatening tone to demonstrate your assertiveness. By doing so, you will have delivered the message in a caring manner.

Practice the Art of Forgiveness

For your mate, this may be a learning curve for them too, as they try to adjust with the child, their ex's posture, and with you. If they make mistakes, talk about it, and let it go. The children may say and do some things as well. Again, communication is key. Take a deep breathe. Forgive. It doesn't mean they should not have consequences. It just means that you should not hold on and keep recounting what has occurred.

Imagine If It Was You or Your Child

Imagine yourself in the stepchild's position, which may be easy if you have been in their situation. How would you like to be treated? What can you do to improve the situation or how they may feel? Being fair goes across the board; to your children, spouse's children, spouse and yourself.

Don't Bad-Mouth the Ex

I don't care how angry you may become, never bad-mouth a child's parents in front of them. Stepparents who make negative comments about their spouse's ex could lead the children to believe that the stepparent wants to replace their parent or set the odds against you when the child tells them what you said. Rather than venting any frustration in the children's presence, talk with friends, a therapist, or consider prayer.

If Things Get Difficult, Don't Retreat

Although it may feel so difficult that you need to physically go on a retreat, don't retreat from your stepfamily's life and growth. It will not always be easy to make it work, but never give up by removing yourself from your stepchild's life, or being absent during their visits. It will be very important that you stand your ground and be comfortable in your own home. If not, the child will see it as a way to get to you. You may find yourself emotionally held captive in an atmosphere where you should feel most secure.

Surprise Custody Of Stepchildren, Another Wild Card!

It can happen. You marry your sweetheart accepting that there are children in the picture, either close, or away in the distance but not in your home full-time. They may have regular short visits, and summers, or may live far away. Basically, your house is your own.

Then suddenly, hello! For any unforeseen reason (death in the family, the child not doing well in school, the custodial parent is going through a major life upheaval, or the custodial parent moves and the child wants to stay in their neighborhood or city), your stepchild is moving in! You will be flooded with emotions; from being panicked and uneasy with the unknown, to overjoyed (if it is something that you and your mate have been desiring).

Your individual experiences and relationship with your stepchild will determine your feelings about the sudden move. More often than not, regardless if you are happy or resistant, your world will be turned upside down, as with any decision of this magnitude. Where you previously held the part-time position, you will now become a primary parental figure in your stepchild's life. If the decision puts you in a negative place, you may find one of your biggest struggles may be the fight to remain gracious. This becomes especially true if the child didn't want to live in your home. The child may be very upset, and you will be the daily recipient of their anger up-close and personal. Keep your cool as best as possible, and vent when your stepchild can't hear you. It won't help to move things into a positive direction if your stepchild overhears you yelling at your spouse about how stressed you are with the changes in your household.

Surprise custody often happens at adolescence when suddenly a teenaged boy towers over his mother; or a girl is really discovering boys and is sneaking out of her room at night. The overwhelmed custodial parent, throwing up his or her hands, sends the child to live with the ex. The rebellious or troubled child, who may have been contemplating the idea of living with the non-custodial parent, is often all too ready to go.

What In the World Do I Do?

We are all creatures of habit. When you uproot a child from their environment, they will need sympathy, concern, and structure, and so do you. Whether the child willingly comes happy about the move, or not, it still is a big transition for everyone. A great deal of adjustment will be in store for you while you help them get acclimated to different surroundings and rules. Your life has suddenly been completely rearranged even if there are other children in the household. It's a different mix now.

Both the biological parent and the stepparent, need to play a prominent role in the adjustment to the newly formed household; reassuring the child that they are wanted and welcomed. Active involvement is a requirement for the child's integration into its new family.

It Is Normal to Feel Overwhelmed

You may feel bad that you are resentful about your life suddenly changing and becoming what seems to be less and less your own. This is not the time to be Mary Poppins in your thinking. The reality is, who wouldn't? Your life is being disrupted. You have responsibilities being required of you that you have to learn to fulfill. It is normal to feel that way. Realize that it may take time for both you and your stepchild to adjust. Make sure to take care of your health, find ways to relieve stress, talk to friends, and have good counsel to get you through.

Even if you may be a little ruffled about having to take on the new full-time responsibility of being a stepparent, try to relate positive feelings to your stepchildren to make them feel wanted. Children are very smart and sensitive. They can tell when they aren't welcome. If the question of them feeling unwanted ever arises, talk with the child. Assure them that you are all in this relationship together.

Some Areas of Focus

School

Communicate the changes in your stepchild's home environment to his/her teachers. The worst thing you can do is to not inform them of the changes in the child's life. Should bad behavior be exhibited during this period of adjustment, they will receive no sympathy, or counseling, because the teachers have no point of reference.

Stay Connected with Their Teachers

Making sure that your stepchild successfully transitions into a new environment will take support from teachers as well as your family.

Stay active in your stepchild's school progression through contact with teachers verbally or via email.

Socializing

Put efforts into helping your stepchild to make new friends and keep in contact with old friends, where the friendships were a positive influence on the child.

Create a Routine

Find out what routine was followed at their other parent's home with regards to homework, dinner, chores, prep for school days, etc. so that you can gain a better understanding of how to incorporate those practices, or alter them to work better for your home.

Contact with Their Other Parent

Keep the other parent informed through email and with pictures. Realize that they are going through an adjustment too, and encourage check-ins with the other parent, if applicable. Encourage your stepchild to stay in touch with their parent, however depending on the current state of their relationship, the frequency of contact will vary.

Strap Up and Enjoy the Ride

Though it may start out rocky, your stepchildren can be some of the biggest blessings in your life. Here are some of the positives that come with being a step parent:

- You have the opportunity to contribute to the successful upbringing of a child.

- If you don't already have children, if you choose to have children, your child will instantly have siblings.

- Your experience can help others (children, parents, other relatives and even ex's).

- You can be a positive statistic to dispel the negative myths about stepparenting.

- Your spouse, will admire your strength and love for their children. They will have a deeper appreciation for your commitment to the relationship.

- You get a dry run on parenting in preparation for your own future children.

For the Biological Parent Whose Spouse is the Stepparent

Do's

- Take time to define the relationship that you would like to have in your new family.

- Share past pertinent information about your child's personality or their life experiences. Give background that will help your new spouse be informed rather than blindsided.

- Show support by recognizing your spouse as someone who matters; an authority figure who is someone you love. Invite the relationship between your children and your spouse.

- Treat the other parent with respect, and demand that your child does as well.

- Take the lead in your parental role, and be open to advice from your spouse.

- Consult your mate on decisions being made about your child. Involve them or at least keep them informed so they feel like a part of their stepchild's life.

- Incorporate 'alone time' with your child as well as family time where you enjoy time as a unit.

- Make your spouse feel appreciated. After all, they are taking on a relationship with your children, a piece of your past that they were not a part of. Always remember that this was a choice for them, and as they adjust, you should be appreciative of their efforts. Giving them something special 'just because' will show them that you are grateful for the way they interact with you and your children.

Don'ts

- Don't expect them to step in and immediately know exactly what to do or say. They may have never been anyone's parent and will need your help in guiding them on this new adventure. Be supportive, and walk them through the process carefully.

- Don't ever imply that because your spouse is not a parent, that they don't understand. Even though in some cases, parental experience does determine how someone reacts to situations, belittling your spouse's experience will only breed resentment for your relationship and the child.

- Don't take the stance that "This is me and my ex's child, we will take care of this. It doesn't concern you." You will be completely excluding your spouse.

As a Stepparent, Never Quit

There will be natural feelings of wanting to withdraw and hide from the whole process. Don't do it! Hang in there! Take the time in between the next visit to strategize, regroup, and try again on your next opportunity. When negative things are directed at you from your stepchildren, it will seem personal and malicious; try not to take it as such. It's really not all about you. Your stepchild may be dealing with a host of feelings that they don't quite know how to express, and are trying their best to adjust as well.

Chapter 12
And Baby Makes 4?

A New Baby, What Now?

For most happy couples, having a new addition to their family is a time of baby bliss. It is a time where an extension of their love has been manifested in the creation of a new life. A new baby usually brings the couple closer, as they now share a child together and find themselves feeling more like a family.

For the person who has been functioning in the role of a stepparent, the new baby may be their first biological child. The person who already has children may be experiencing having a child for the first time inside a marital union.

For the sake of example, take a father who comes into the marriage with children he had very young, and a wife who has no children. Whether the father found himself feeling unprepared, financially deficient, immature, or in an undesirable relationship, the wonderful children that were produced came into an environment that may have not been ideal. Because the father is now older and married (hopefully more prepared), the addition of a new child may be very welcomed, as well as the feelings associated with their spouse's pregnancy.

Telling the Kids
The way you tell the children about the new baby will differ depending on the age of the children and their individual personalities.

Older children probably have already had thoughts that there may be a child entering the picture, and have come to terms with the idea. Their thoughts may oscillate between resentment, excitement, and even anxiety, depending on how they have chosen to accept the new marriage.

Younger children may be a bit excited that they will have a baby sister or brother; someone that will look up to them, and that they can care for. The key to making sure they don't feel threatened is to include them into the whole "new baby" event. Explaining to the young child that they will be a big brother or sister, that they will need to be a helper, and that this is "their" brother or sister, usually takes away the idea they will be pushed out of the family or feelings of being replaced. Nevertheless, know that as soon as you tell the child, in their excitement, they will immediately tell their other parent that they are having a new sibling.

So Should The Ex Be Formally Told About The New Baby?

In most relationships between children and their non-custodial parent, the parent and child have a relationship that is kept separate from the other parent. Because they live in two entirely different households, the two parents individually raise the child, and only come together on matters that call for the attention of both parents. Consequently, what happens on the visitation weekends is a separate world from the other parent until the child invites the custodial parent in by telling them what they did while at dad's or mom's house.

Although every family relationship is different, in most cases, it is perfectly acceptable to hear the news of the new baby from the child in their weekend recap after visiting the non-custodial parent's home. This holds especially true if the relationship between the two parents may be estranged. If one or both of the parents are not exactly at a place of calm communication, to call and tell the other parent that you and your new spouse are having a new baby may be something they would rather not hear, especially from you.

However, if the child is having a difficult time adjusting to the new marriage, it might be a good idea, to give the other parent a heads up as to what you will be telling him or her so they can be supportive to their child. Again, the maturity level of the other parent will determine whether telling your child about the new baby will be helpful or a hindrance, and if the ex's assistance is needed in telling the child.

If you feel like you should tell the ex, the parent should do so with the tone they would use for a courtesy call (like you would give to an employer) – just FYI!

A Conversation With the Stepparent Having a Baby For the First Time

It's a Different World
Parenting and Step parenting – there is a difference!

Now that you have become a new parent, one of the most obvious things you will be aware of is your natural innate feelings toward your new child, and how they differ from those you feel for your stepchild(ren).

As a stepparent you inherited a relationship with your spouses child. Because you love your mate, the love you feel for them spills over as you learn to love your stepchild. Depending on the age of the child and circumstances in which you and your stepchild's relationship is being cultivated, you may have had to create a reservoir from which to draw these parental feelings.

With stepparenting, you can find yourself always striving to make it work; trying to have them like you as you get to know each other. The relationship is an arranged one that requires work from everyone involved to create a sense of normalcy. However, when you become a new parent to your own child, you don't have to "work" to gain their love or to love them; it just is. When a mother has their biological child, immediately the parent carries and physically nurtures their child entirely. The bond between the parent and child is already an internal connection.

For many stepparents, having their own child changes their relationship with their stepchildren, and how they relate to them positively and negatively; at least if only negative in the early adjustment period with the new baby.

There are a lot of factors coming into play with the way the stepparent feels during this pregnancy, especially if the stepparent is a woman who happened to marry a man with children. As a new mother, the steparent is also experiencing the natural hormonal changes a woman goes through during pregnancy and post pregnancy. The slightest bit of confusion or drama from the baby's mama or their child, which before was tolerable, may now seem to be extremely heightened and unacceptable.

Some stepparents may feel they have been fair and gracious through the ups and downs of dealing with the stepchild and the ex; but now, in this special time of their life, they want it to be a moment unshared and drama-free; a moment with them, their spouse, and their new baby. The point to remember is that it is very natural to feel this way. Although your mate may have a child, this may be your first baby with your husband or wife. It is natural for you to want this child to have the normal attention that surrounds a new baby.

And yes, the experience may feel different when it's your first child, but not your mate's first child. You may feel a little cheated that they have already had their first parental experience.

The best way to deal with your feelings is to talk about it even prior to conception. Talk about how you want life to be during the pregnancy, and try to plan ahead. Discuss how you two will handle things if your stepchild happens to be with you when it's time to deliver, and how you would feel about them being there. Plan for everything you can think may become a concern. At least you and your mate will be aware of your expectations, fears and concerns, and be able to effectively deal with them should they occur.

Some Feelings Of the Couple Expecting Their First Child Together

———— ✿ ————

The Positives

We Finally Have Our Child Together, We Are "Official"

For the stepparent who is having their first child, gaining the "official" parent status can help bring validation of their relationship.

The stepparent may feel that they and their spouse finally have a child together, and their own family where everyone can participate. Whether they admit it or not, marrying someone who already has children may make the stepparent who has no child with their spouse feel as if the ex has a bond with them that they do not. Back in Chapter 1, we talked about the natural order of family, and how when you put the "cart before the horse" by having children with someone that you do not marry, you cause confusion with a future marriage. When you decide to get married, you carry your past relationship(s), and more importantly, a child you created with your ex, into your new marriage. It becomes a difficult circumstance for you, the ex, your future mate, and especially the children; both prior and the future children you may have when you get married.

As a stepparent, even the nicest person would have to admit that there could be insecurity when it comes to that harsh reality that you are "not a parent." Comments echoed by the ex, implied by your spouse or others, or maybe even your own voice that says, "you won't understand because you aren't a parent" can be haunting.

All of that changes once you have your own child. Not only will you have the experience of having your own child together, you will also do so inside a marriage where you will have the support of your spouse, family, and friends.

Stepparents Can Make Great Parents
They've already had on the job training! One advantage to having the role of a stepparent prior to having your own child is that you have had some previous parenting experience, so you're not going in completely cold turkey! Your maternal or paternal muscles have been in training!

A New Child Can Knit Everyone Together
Children, parents, and extended families find themselves uniting because the new child will be a part of all of them. Sometimes it can be a badge of respect even to your stepchild's parent! In the eyes of the stepchild's parent, the spouse can seem more like "a parent", and be given more respect now that they have given birth to their own child. The new baby brings a sense of completeness to the entire family.

The New Parent May Find They Feel Closer to Their Stepchildren After Having Their Own Child
Because they are a parent to their own baby, the parent's parental instincts are fine-tuned. Overall, this means that they are more sensitive to children, including their stepchildren. Many times the stepchild's positive reaction to their new sibling will make the stepparent's feelings for their stepchild grow. Having a baby allows you to see the similarities in both your stepchildren and your child because they share a parent. Your new baby may even

physically look like the stepchild, making you realize that you all are connected.

The Negatives

Share, Share, Share!
Some Negative Feelings the New Mother May Experience
One of the things that the new parent will have to deal with is coming to grips with the fact that your child will have to 'share' their life with your stepchildren. I think that every couple probably considers what will come with having a new child; time, money, and emotional commitment. When you are experiencing your first biological child, you will be faced with the reality that all of the fore- mentioned elements have to be shared with other children outside of your marriage. Although you realize that those children deserve to be cared for like any other child; you will have to share your new child's resources and time with other children outside of your marriage.

Because the entire blended family experience is shared from the beginning, it can lead to feelings of resentment you never experienced at this level, before the addition of a new baby. Your natural, parental instincts to provide, protect, and nurture, immediately kick in. Now when you may have to buy clothing within a certain budget, or you want more family time but it's little Johnny's weekend to visit, it becomes an issue because the money and time is not just yours to give, but your new baby. For families on a very tight budget, imagine the feeling you may have when your new baby is constantly in need of new clothes because they're going through a growth spurt. You may not be able to buy them what they need because you will have just spent $1000 in child support payments! It's enough to make an eyebrow rise at the very least!

The good news is that as you learn to juggle, balance, shift, and adjust –it usually gets better. If you are the stepmother giving birth, you will eventually fit back into your jeans. Work a little harder to balance the expenses, continue falling in love with your new little one, and learn to deal with your new world.

Feeling Overwhelmed

You may often find yourself feeling overwhelmed with the demands of a new baby along with stepparenting. Somehow, between not sleeping, early morning feedings, and changing diapers, your tolerance level is low. When you are feeling overwhelmed, don't allow yourself to feel guilty for not being able to show your stepchild as much attention as they had before the baby. Having a child is a big adjustment, and it's natural to feel like you are pulling double-duty physically and emotionally. This is the time where your mate will need to step in and help more with your stepchild. If you usually did an activity with the child, have your mate do it in your place. Children associate feeling needed with being wanted. Make them feel needed. Having a talk with the stepchildren about everyone pitching in to help with the new baby may also alleviate some of the pressure you may be feeling.

Jealousy From the Ex

A new baby has a way of affirming a marriage and brings finality to all former relationships. It solidifies that you now have an official family with someone else. The ex may feel they need to protect what they feels is theirs; their child and their feelings. This may be the time when you experience some retaliation from the ex because of their emotions, insecurities, and lobbying to make sure their child is not forgotten. During this delicate time, the main concern should not be with convincing the ex, but spent reassuring your stepchild that you love them. It is the child's feelings that are most important, not the ex's.

Don't Play Favorites

You don't even want to start with this one! Once you and your spouse have children of your own, the goal is to be as fair as possible. Although you will have an innate attachment to your own child, when disciplining and performing day-to-day activities, you should make every attempt to be fair. This means that when the baby becomes older, your birth child should not get special privileges, or get less disciplined because he or she lives in the house with you. When your stepchild is visiting, you should make every attempt to treat them fairly and not favor either. The same should hold true (watch out for reverse guilt trips) when the visiting child does something wrong; they should not get special leniencies because they are not there all the time. To do so, will send a message to the non-resident child of unfairness, and being favored as well.

Some Tips On How to Create Balance

- Communicate your feelings with your spouse and work out a plan that ensures everyone gets the attention they need during pregnancy and after the baby arrives.

- For Mom: Be sure to take time for moments of relaxation; visit a spa, take in a movie, or have lunch out by yourself or with friends.

- For the Stepparent: On weekends of visitation, plan an outing for you and the baby to give your spouse and your stepchild their own time together, but be sure to also initiate time with the new baby and your stepchildren.

- Make references to the stepchild of them being a big brother or sister. Doing this allows them to feel responsible, and closer to their sibling.

A Conversation For the Parent Whose Spouse Is Having Their First Child

Be Sensitive to the Fact That This Is Your Spouse's First Child

Even if this is not your first child, it is your first time as a parent with your spouse. Try to experience everything fresh, through their eyes, as if it were your first time too. Please don't keep bringing up what you did with your other children when they were this age, (or if a male), when your other child's mother was pregnant, unless you want to be sleeping on the couch indefinitely! The most important thing to remember is that your mate will want to share this moment with you, and not feel like they are playing second or even third fiddle to your past relationships – especially because you are married to them.

The Adjustment Period

Realize that when the child is first born, until you both get the hang of the new baby, there will be an adjustment period before your mate kicks back in to complete stepparent mode. Your spouse will be adjusting to being a biological parent for the first time, and juggling parenting to your child as well. Immediately after the child is born, the parent will have a host of emotions and feelings as they adjust to having a child of their own child. It is natural that there will be some growing pains as they shifts from stepparent to full- time parent.

Help Out

Help take the load off of your spouse by assisting any way you can. When your child is visiting, take the lead in creating a good visit, especially in the areas where your spouse may have contributed more. Giving them time away to unwind, and helping out will lighten their feelings of being overwhelmed.

Finding Balance and Enough Love For Everyone

The new spouse may also feel that because the new child is in the house everyday, when the stepchild comes to visit, the other parent drops everything to be with their visiting child, often overcompensating for them having a "new baby". It will be very important that you learn to balance your time and energy so that no one feels left out. One of the best ways to do so is to bring everyone together so the time is equally shared, and also create personal time with the visiting child. Strive to make your visiting child feel included and a part of the family.

Having a new baby with your spouse should be an opportunity to add even more beauty to your relationship. Enjoy this experience within your marriage, and help your children to enjoy your happiness.

Chapter 13
I Said "I Do" Before

It Didn't and Now I'm Saying It Again, Except We Both Have Children!

The Merriam Webster dictionary states that a blended family is: "a family that includes children of a previous marriage of one's spouse or from both (the woman and man)". Another definition would be "a family unit consisting of two previously married parents and the children of their former marriages."

It is reported that there are now more combinations of blended families than there are of traditional nuclear families. From individuals that divorce, to couples who were never married, the term "blended" covers a lot of territory, and no longer is primarily associated with marriage. In this chapter, we will specifically be addressing the couple who both have children from previous relationships, are in preparation for, or are planning to be married living under the same roof.

Establishing a blended family when both individuals have children requires both people are first prepared to be married (see Chapter 8 Pre- Marital Counseling). Once the couple is positive they are ready to commit, they have to realize blending families and building strong family bonds will require effort from everyone involved. As families merge, everyone will need time to adjust, and make an effort to get to know each other. Patience will have to be practiced as the new family unit is formed.

Another important factor will be the couple's ability to learn from their past mistakes in previous relationships, especially in cases where there is a divorce or where there has been a lengthy relationship. According to the Academy of Matrimonial Attorneys, at least 67 percent of second marriages fail. What are the reasons? People don't deal with the issues or heal the personal wounds that played a role in the demise of their first marriage before remarrying. The added pressure of raising stepchildren causes more conflict than unstable marriages can handle.

The couple getting married will have to form a secure, united bond as they handle the challenges that come with a blended family. It will also be very important that you communicate the goals and expectations for the new, blended family, both with each other and your children.

Below are my 7 Steps for Blended Family Success for couples to explore before blending a new family, as well as tips you can incorporate into your new Blended Family.

Step #1: Before You Blend, Put In a Little Prep Work
Honestly Discuss Why Your Other Relationship(s) Failed

Know and understand what you contributed to the failure of your marriage or relationship. It will be critical that you make every effort to avoid making the same mistakes twice, especially when a breakup would destroy an even more complicated family. If you need further help before you get married, seek counseling or study privately to assure that you are healed from your previous relationship. Decide that this will be a fresh start, and elect to not bring any of the old hang-ups or disappointments you have encountered in your previous relationships to your new marriage.

Points to Consider:
- Why do you feel this relationship would be different?
- How are you different now? What did you learn?

Step #2: Discuss Each Others Parenting Styles and Children

Talk with your potential spouse about how they are currently parenting their children. Get a feel for their take on discipline, respect, and communication so you can see exactly where they are coming from and if it will mesh with the way that you raise your children. This will be very important because both of you will need to be on the same page in order to have one consistent parenting pattern for all of your children. When you disagree about a component in the other parent's parenting style, talk about your concerns without being judgmental. If you don't address the issues now, you can end up being resentful of your spouse if they make a decision that doesn't mirror how you would handle a situation.

This will be the time that you want to see just how good the two of you are at coming up with solutions together, and if each can allow another person to be a parental figure to their children. If there are problems cooperating in this stage beware; it could indicate what is in store should you marry. If you can't agree now, most likely, it's not going to get any better when children are added to the equation.

Points to Consider:

- Talk about your own parenting style and be honest.

- Discuss different parenting/discipline scenarios and how you would address the problem.

- Where do you feel you could improve as a parent?

- Honestly talk about your child's personality. If your daughter's mouth is out of control, tell her. If your son has a heart of gold, but is very sensitive and possessive, discuss it.

- After hearing the parent's views on parenting, discuss anything the other parent may do in their parenting that you question, or don't agree with and explain why.

- What role, if any, does their other biological parent play in their lives?

Step #3: Discuss the Blending of the Families with Your Children Before It Happens

Once you are sure that you are getting married, you will need to prepare your child for the new additions to the family so that they have an understanding of how their life will be affected. Allow them to openly discuss their feelings, and be available to answer their questions. If you have been seeing the potential spouse for any amount of time; the two of you getting married may be something that your children have already assumed was going to happen. Usually, when a child can see their parent is happy, they have a better outlook on embracing the changes that come along with that happiness.

Points to Consider:

- Talk to your children about the potential for your new blended family to become a reality.

- Discuss their feelings. Respect their concerns. What may seem trivial to you, may be monumental to them.

- Assure them that this is not taking away anything from their family, but in fact, you will be gaining more people in your family.

- Let them know that although it may be an adjustment, putting in effort to make it work is half of the battle.

Step #4: Get the Children to Know Each Other and Your Potential Spouse

The timeframe in which you actually decide to introduce your potential spouse to your children will be an individual decision, but definitely should not be done until you are positive that this person is going to be around for the long haul. Your children have already been through a lot with the separation of their parents, and they don't need to meet multiple people and their families that may not be around tomorrow.

When the introduction is made, observe how your children interact with your potential spouse and any children they have. Be sure to discuss later your observations with your potential spouse, and compare notes. Communicate to your potential spouse that it will be important for them to be themselves and be natural. Young children are usually a good judge of character. They know when a person is sincere or genuine. Like any other newly formed relationship, it will require time for each party to get to know the other. Initially everyone will be feeling the other out. Give it time, and allow the relationships to naturally form and grow.

Meeting the Potential "New" Family

- Decide with your potential spouse when everyone who is going to part of the 'new' family should meet.

- In some cases it may be best to introduce the new potential spouse first, and then their children separately or at another time.

- Plan family date nights with both families in a laid back atmosphere to allow them to socialize without pressure.

- Find out what everyone likes (food, movie, activity). Try to choose some of those things each time you go out, so that both families feel included.

- Encourage but don't push the children to like each other. Just as children take a moment to connect with their classmates, (this is no different). Kids will be kids.

Step #5: Establish the New Home Order and Develop a Blended Family Plan

It essential that the couple commit to being a team and working as a unit once married. It will be very important to embrace each other as partners in parenting. Having a plan for how your new home life will look will be necessary if you desire peace in your home. It is not about one person coming in and enforcing their ideas and agenda without consideration for how things have been in the past. It is about both parents merging together to make the best family experience for everyone.

Both parents must fully understand how all the children are accustomed to doing things. He/she should not make any disruptive changes, but be sensitive as to how to grandfather in change. For some, the transition may be easier than others. For example. one set of children may actually fill a void for the other: i.e. the younger child wanting an older brother, or a little sister. In this case, the child may be excited and ready for them to become a family.

All situations are different, but the key is that everyone respect each other, and put forth the effort to adapt and embrace all involved.

Developing Your Blended Family Plan

- Set up your families house rules. Make sure you combine rules that are important to both of you.

- Determine how you will enforce rules that will be well-suited to both parenting styles.

- Make sure you write down discipline and reward procedures.

- Set up a consistent day and time to sit down and discuss the happenings in the house, or to talk about any disagreements that have come up.

- Take time to discuss any conflict you think may arise in the future.

- List routines and activities everyone can do as a family to help the blending process.

- Write down things you can you do as a couple that will keep the romantic fire burning. Your love for each other is the foundation of your new blended family. *If that love isn't nurtured, your marriage and family will suffer.*

- List what you can do to meet family member's emotional needs. Emotional needs should be a priority. Take care of yourself as an individual and each other.

- Evaluate the finances you are going to need to support your new blended family. Draft a realistic household budget with allowances for the children, so you don't overlook any of the household member's needs.

Step #6: Defining and Supporting the New Roles
What Will Your Role Be In Your Blended Family?

Until now, each parent has led separate lives with their children where they were an authority in their households. For example, take the child of a single or divorced mother who is getting married. That child may have never had a father in her life (or with little involvement), and be accustomed to it just being her and her mom. When a new parental figure comes in, the child may still refer to their parent as their authority figure, and the new parent is not respected as a joint authority figure in the household. This is why it is very important that both parents communicate with their children about the respect they expect their children to have for their new mate. The new mate has to also step up to the plate and assert that role. If the mother steps back in when the stepfather is trying to display his position as man of the house, the child will never respect the new family union, and there will be an "us and them" mindset. The husband will feel disrespected, and the mother will feel they are being placed in the middle. It will take time for the child to adjustment, but positive reinforcement will allow the child to see the flow of the household, and they will begin to adapt positively when they are treated with love, understanding, and respect.

Foster positive relationships within a newly blended family by taking time to talk and listen to all involved in the new family unit. Every member of a blended family needs to know and feel that their opinions matter and are valued.

Step #7: Encourage Family Time
Gently Encourage Strong Sibling Relationships

In a traditional family, to get along is sometimes difficult between brothers and sisters. When you add in more parents and siblings, it can be challenging for them to express themselves as they deal with the possible feelings of feeling hurt and competition.

Parents and children should make every attempt to build strong relationships between stepsiblings and half-siblings. Having them celebrate their similarities, automatically provides them with common ground. Parents should plan activities and incorporate family time that allow them to begin seeing each other as a family unit. In a nuclear family, relationships grow over time. This relationship is no different.

Step #8: Create Blended Family Fun

Find activities that the whole family can enjoy that will cover all of the age groups represented in your family.
Here are some ideas:

>*"Game Night" at Your Home*
>Choose games everyone can play, or create different game stations within the same room if there is a drastic difference in ages. The key here is that everyone is in one room playing games together.

>*Have a "Create Your Own Pizza" Night*
>Cooking together offers opportunities for preschoolers to get messy and older children to exert some authority

by choosing what they want on their pizza. What can bring a family together more than a great pizza and sharing a meal?

Plan a Family Trip
Whether it's a two-day road trip, or an extended getaway, vacations are always welcomed. Take suggestions from everyone and choose multiple locations so every one gets a turn at going where they want to go. (within reason)

Swim Dates
The swimming pool also encourages togetherness. Plan swim dates for the whole family to enjoy.

Step #9: Make Time for All of the Children's Important Events

With all of your blended family living in one household, you probably have a ridiculous calendar of events to keep track of everyone's activities and commitments.

Ask your child and her teachers or coaches what are the most important events to attend. That way, if your children have events that overlap, you and your spouse can split up to attend both, and have a little leeway if you don't make every activity.

Some Final Blended Family Tips

Don't Expect Everything to Be Perfect

A blended family is still the dissolution of another family, so don't try and make the new family unit immediately perfect. As in any family, there will be disagreements and opportunities for strife. A healthy family will form when everyone's goal is working together, sharing themselves and accepting each other.

Give Love

Make sure that both you and your mate show love and affection to all the children, not just to each person's set of biological children. Give everyone hugs. Pat everyone on the back. Show them that you are all in this together.

Institute Individual Quality Time

It will be natural during the beginning for the couple to unintentionally attempt to force everyone to do everything together. Allow the children to have individual time, even time with their parent. It is still important for the biological parent and their child to share quality time so that the child doesn't feel that they have gained a new family, but lost their parent.

Same Rules Across the Board

Maintain consistent rules for all the children. Set a standard for everyone. Should they fall short, enforce the same type of consequences. Make sure all children do their fair share around the house by incorporating chores and giving responsibilities to each person. Demonstrating consistency with the rules, chores, and responsibilities should help to prevent favoritism, animosity, and encourage the development of mutual respect.

Teach the Children to Respect Each Other

Talking about each other, teasing, or being mean only hurts the people the act is directed to, it strains the relationships. Everyone should be taught to have respect for each other. Parents have to demonstrate their respect for each other and the children to be good models for their family.

Allow Children to Have Their Own Personal Space

Combining two households also means blending two of everything. Your house may quickly become crowded, bursting at the seams. Be sure that every child has their own space. It could be a special shelf, part of a closet, or a couple of drawers in a chest.

Designating that it is their own will make them feel secure and a part of the family.

Respect Each Other's Property

Once the kids have their own space, make sure that everyone respects each other's territory. No one should take anything that they don't first ask permission to use from the owner. If the child goes away to visit their other parent, they should come back and find that their things are in tact, and have not been disturbed.

Surround Yourself with Support

Reach out to grandparents, church counselors, support groups or community-based programs to help your blended family adjust. The key is finding individuals who specifically can identify with blended families and the issues they face.

Commit to Being the Best Person You Can Everyday

With time, love, respect, and sharing, your blended family can be the greatest blessing you will ever experience as all of the children grow into responsible men and women. The right motives, love, determination, and faith can transform a difficult situation into a long-term, rewarding relationship.

Part Three

Moving on, Growing Up, Realizing That We're All In This Together

Chapter 14

Imagine That!

Cooperative Parenting

At the beginning of a relationship that has ended, the parents may find it very difficult to communicate with each other, or even be in the same space for the smallest amount of time. As time passes, people heal, mature and move on with their lives. The tension shared diminishes to a point where the parents can focus their attention on the bond they share, their child. The parents may have also entered into new relationships, even married; which now gives the child (ren) stepparents who will be contributing to their growth.

As the parents and their new spouses settle into their lives, there will be more opportunities for communication without contention. Everyone can focus their energy to raise the child together. And while this is the ideal scenario, the time frame will vary for every set of parents. Some may be mature enough to relate to each other from the beginning, whereas, others may never move on with their lives, remaining angry and bitter well into the child's adult life.

> *Parenting and nurturing your children is the most important job you will ever have.*

If parents can work together in a peaceful manner, you can all help to raise a healthy and secure child.

> *Make a decision to put your personal issues aside in order to give your best to your children.*

They not only deserve your support, they will appreciate and respect you when they become adults and can recognize your unselfishness.

The best way to get through your eighteen years and be good parents together is to sit down and build a parenting plan. In a parenting plan, parents work to maintain an amicable relationship for the sake of their children. Parenting plans, also called "cooperative parenting plans" or "parenting partnerships," are gaining popularity because of the benefits they offer to the children. Most experts agree that children adjust better to separation and divorce when both parents continue to be active in their lives, creating a map for their child's success and emotional well-being. In some states, it is a mandatory part of the divorce process to file a parenting plan.

While some parents deeply resent the other parent, if they can put their differences aside long enough to create the cooperative plan for their child's life, it will more than pay off when the goals of the plan are reached through their child's stability, character, and success. Through your attitude, actions and parenting partnership, your children will recognize that they are more important than the reasons your relationship ended and understand that your love for them prevails even under changing circumstances.

A good co-parenting plan should be flexible to allow for changing needs and circumstances. This chapter will guide you through the process of building your parenting plan which will be one of the greatest, long-lasting gifts you can give your children.

Benefits of a Parenting Plan

Children Whose Parents Have a Cooperative Parenting Plan and Relationship Gain the Following Benefits:

- Similar rules in both households will establish stability in their lives.

- The children will feel secure and loved from seeing that even though their parents are not together, they can continue to parent collaboratively, which will enable the child to adapt better to the parent's separation.

- By the parents demonstrating teamwork, children will learn how to solve problems, cooperate and be flexible.

- The children will benefit from the parents planning for their development, which will put them in a position to win in life.

The Shared Parenting Plan Should Address:

- Etiquette between the parents and how they will communicate with each other

- Establishment and maintainence of similar discipline and household rules

- Preparation and expectations for education & college

- Long-term financial commitments such as life insurance, college savings

- Children's medical needs or concerns

- Holidays, special events, summer camps, and activities

Preparing Your Thoughts For Your Input On the Parenting Plan

Successful co-parenting requires open lines of communication. One of the most effective ways to improve communication and understanding between parents and their new spouses is a meeting to talk about raising the children. Make an effort to use these tips to set aarms-length atmosphere to your meetings. This will allow you to keep yourself at an emotional distance from your Ex.

Tips for Conducting Successful Co-Parenting Meetings

Set a Business-Like Tone

Treat your meetings and conduct yourselves in the way in which you would act in a business meeting. To a certain degree, raising your child is like a business partnership where your personal feelings are checked at the front door, and you are expected to make rational decisions. You and the other parent(s) have one objective: to raise your child to the best of your collaborative ability. The truth is you may not like everyone and coming together and talking may be difficult, but the success and health of your child relies on your ability to work together towards one common goal – the long-term success of your child.

Meet Every Three Months

Commit to have a meeting every three months. This could coincide with report cards markings, which allows enough time to see the results of the implementation of your plan. Be flexible and adjust the meetings as necessary. For example, in a case where you may need to handle an adjustment in behavior or school performance, more contact may be needed. When you regularly come together, you will convey the message to your children that they matter. In the beginning it may be difficult. However if you keep your focus centered on what you have in common, you will find the meetings will get easier with time.

Communicate Via the Phone and E-mail

Do not feel as if you have to pull up chairs, look each other in the eyes and sip coffee to have a meeting. You do not have to meet in person. This takes a lot of pressure off the parents who want to be there for their child but may not be comfortable in such close proximity to their ex. Using the telephone or e-mail is completely fine. If you discover another way to review the plan, that's fine too. Use whatever method is most productive for everyone.

Use an Agenda

Topics like school progress, behavior and schedules will be discussed at each meeting. By creating an agenda, not only will you organize your thoughts, but it will allow for a more productive meeting. Create a standard form that includes all the topics you want to discuss regularly, leaving room for additional items that come up. Complete and distribute the form prior to your meeting so that both parents will have the opportunity to review it. It will be very important that the parents take the time to prepare for the meeting so the meeting can be as productive as possible in the shortest amount of time.

Keep Your Focus On the Child Period

The entire purpose of having the meeting is the success of your child. Keep that in mind when you communicate with each other. Make a conscious choice to set your feelings aside and stay focused on the child's needs during these meetings. It is not the time for personal feelings, child support issues, or rehashing conflicts in your relationship. If those issues need to be addressed, choose a separate time from your co-parenting meetings.

Set a time limit for your meetings. Lingering too long on subjects will leave the gate open for confrontations.

Very Important:
Make a copy of the issues and items to be discussed. Send it to the other parent at least two weeks prior to your meeting. Confirm that they have received the information. Set a date and time for the meeting.

Developing Your Parenting Plan

There are three separate agendas inside of the plan.

Part One - The Initial Meeting
It should only be held once, when you initially institute your co-parenting meetings. This meeting should cover general co-parenting etiquette, guidelines for how you will relate to each other, as well as general ideas and goals.

Part Two - The Operational Section
It should be a meeting held every three months. The operational section covers the things you will always discuss such as grades, behavior, schedules and activities.

Part Three - The Long-Term Goals Section
It should be a meeting held annually. This meeting will discuss the child's future, and is based upon future goals and potential changes.

Part One – The Initial Objective Meeting

Building the Character of Your Child

Both Parents Should Individually Make a List of the Things That They Deem Most Important to Teach the Child
More often than not, they will realize they share the same thoughts on what is important for the development of their child. By doing this, most parents will find that this helps to initiate teamwork because they have a common goal.

Discuss the Household Rules

This is especially important since the children will be living in two different households. Although there may be some differences, the parents should try to remain consistent so that the child can remain stable and better adjust to being in both households.

When Disciplining in One Household, the Other Parent Should Agree to Support the Other's Rules

If the child is being punished in one household, the other parent should follow through with the punishment when the child visits. This can be especially hard when the parent may only see the child every other weekend, but to not follow the punishment removes the consequences for a child's actions. For example, if one parent tells the child no video games until his or her behavior improves in school, the other parent should enforce the same rule.

When Conflicts Arise, Be Mature Enough to Discuss and Compromise

Don't allow personal problems between adults to compromise your ability to be able to communicate and be effective parents. You can be emotionally distant from your ex without conflict. Find middle ground and agree for the sake of the child.

Never Argue About Differences in Parenting Styles or Anything for That Matter in Front of the Child

No one will ever do things exactly as you would – especially your ex! Your parenting style is not theirs and vice-versa.

Choose to handle any issues you have with the ex privately, not in front of the child. When the child is present, show mutual respect and be as polite as possible to one another.

Agree

- Agree not to criticize each other.
- Agree not to use the children to deliver messages or information to or from your ex.

- Agree not to discuss custody issues or money issues in front of the children.

Part Two - Operational

Communication and Daily Living

Schedules

Discuss any changes or requested modifications of the visitation order due to any other school related activities. Both parents should strive to adhere to the specifics of the visitation order at all times. Activities can occasionally come up that may alter the schedule. Should it be a concern, discuss that in this section. In addition, discuss any important school functions and/or events that may require both parents' attendance.

Discuss Your Child's Academic Progress

Discuss what has been happening in school from teacher concerns special standardized tests, to homework. If there are concerns about their academics, devise a strategy that will help your child improve their grades. Suggest tips that may have helped in the past. Explore getting outside help like tutors, or mentors if more help is necessary than the parents can provide.

Discuss Your Child's Behavioral Progress

When trying to rectify or eliminate a behavior, the proposed solution must be reinforced in both households. Discuss what you are doing in your home to help your child overcome a behavior, and be open to suggestions from your ex.

For example, if you're limiting talking on the phone to 30 minutes every other day, the other parent shouldn't allow the child to have an hour. The parent initiating the behavior modification should discuss the reason for this restriction or rule and ask the other parent to be cooperative about following the rule in their home.

Concerns You Have

Discuss any concerns that you have about your child. Is your son not socializing well? Is your daughter hanging around and talking about one particular boy a little too much? Share these concerns with each other so that you can provide your child with support and guidance.

Come to a Consensus or Agreement

Record any action plans you have made in order to incorporate them in the child's life after the meeting.

Items to Be Discussed For the Next Meeting

If you did not have the time to discuss something, or during the meeting other topics came up that require more discussion, jot it down for the next meeting's agenda.

Summarize the Meeting

Summarize what you've discussed in the meeting and send a copy to the other parent. This will help you to see what you have accomplished. It also helps to assure that both of you came away from the meeting with a similar understanding of what has been successful and what remains to be done.

Part Three - The Long Term Plan

Future Goals And Life Changes

Education

- Discuss your views with each other about major educational decisions (for example, whether to change schools, or whether to take advanced level courses).

- Before it is time for the child to go to high school, (preferably in 7th grade), discuss where they should attend school (i.e. college prep, charter, performing arts, private).

College

- Discuss any plans for higher education as in technical trade schools, universities, or internships.

- Establish when you will begin preparing them for standardized tests, such as the ACT and SAT.

- Discuss any other preparation such as college tours, or summer study programs.

- Discuss how you will assist them in applying for scholarships, financial aid, preparing and reviewing their college resume.

College Savings

- What financial arrangements need to be made now for your child's higher education?

- Can both parents contribute to the cost of college? If so, how should you share these costs? Should you invest the savings?

- What restrictions, if any, should be placed on your duty to contribute to college (e.g., paying for public college only or paying only if they receive an established grade point average)?

- Not every child will be able to find free money for college.

  - Will you be willing to co-sign for an educational loan?

  - Will your credit be good enough? If not, work on this now.

- What advance savings arrangements, if any, should you agree to make to pay for college?

- What general savings (that is, in addition to or separate from college costs) should be set-aside for your children?

- Who should contribute to savings, and who should manage them?

- What is your Plan B, in case neither of you can afford to send the child to college?

Athletics & Extra Curricular Activities

- Are there particular sports that are particularly important to your child? Are either of you more oriented toward one sport than the other?

- Are there particular sports in which your child should not participate, or should not participate until a given age? If so, what are they, and why?

- Agree how you want to participate in school events.

- Agree on if or how you would like to participate in any extracurricular events.

- Agree on if or how you would like to participate in teachers conferences.

- Discuss on any other important things to have your child involved in (i.e. scouts, or a service oriented group).

Special Events

- Share your thoughts on how you want to participate or contribute to the special events that happen in the child's life, such as Prom, Sweet 16, Homecoming, Graduation Activities, other Special Events, and Baptism.

- Declare a child's events neutral ground. Everyone will behave and treat each other respectfully.

Spiritual Life

- What sort of spiritual involvement should your child receive?

- What level of attendance in church is important to you both?

- At what age would you like your child to make a decision to join a church or establish a relationship with God?

- How do you plan to aid in their spiritual development?

- Should the child be involved in youth groups and mission trips?

Sex Education

- In what way will the two of you talk with your children about sex, abstinence, and sexually transmitted diseases?

- At an appropriate age (to be determined by the parents), this would be a good opportunity to encourage their awareness of the disadvantages of having children outside of marriage, and divorce. Assure them that although their existence is not a mistake, there are consequences for their decisions and rewards for being sexually responsible and abstaining.

- What age is appropriate to discuss these topics?

Medical Needs

- Honestly discuss your child's health and any concerns or problems

- Agree to contact the other parent immediately should there be a need of emergency care.

- Should there be a need, agree to transfer medications to the other parent, not your child, at trade-off times. Include written instructions on dosage and side effects with the medication.

Proximity & Relocation

- How close should the parents live while the child is growing up?

- Do you intend to continue living in the same area until the child is an adult?

- If you're separated by distance, who should pay for the children to travel? Should there be an adjustment in child support?

- Is there an agreed upon time when you feel custody should change? (As in when the male son reaches puberty/ teenager) If so at what age?

- Will the ultimate decision to change residences be left to the child at a designated age?

Come to a Consensus or Agreement

Take a moment to record any decisions you've made together so you don't forget to incorporate them in between meetings.

Items to be Discussed For the Next Meeting

If you did not have the time to discuss something, or in your meeting other subtopics came up that require more discussion, jot it down and put it on the next meeting's agenda.

Summarize the Meeting

Summarize what you've discussed today and email a copy to the other parent. This will help you to see what was accomplished. It also helps to assure that both of you came away from the meeting with a similar understanding of what took place.

IMAGINE THAT!

Decide When you Will Revisit the Plan

Have a yearly meeting before school starts, to coincide with the new school year. Before you schedule the meeting, review the previous year's plan. It may not be necessary to review the long-term goals section every year, because there may not have been any major changes. Still, make a point of setting a tentative date. At least a week prior to that date, take inventory of the things previously discussed in the Long Term Goals section to decide if it is necessary to meet on the scheduled date.

Realize that you are simply forecasting what you would like to happen. Understand that during the years of the child growing and becoming more of themselves, certain goals may change, so allow for any growth and changes that may occur.

Ending Thoughts

Once you get your eighteen-year-old successfully off to college or into the job market, you will be proud that you ALL put yourselves aside, and decided to do what was necessary to make it work. All of the pain, meetings, and hard work will be worth it when you can look at 'everyone's' child as they walk across the high school stage and into their own destiny; a destiny you helped to make secure and healthy for them, despite your circumstances.

Just know that your job as a parent doesn't stop, it never does. If you've done a good job, you have well equipped him or her with what they need to make good decisions as a productive member of society. They will have learned from their own family experiences to make good choices in life, love, marriage, and truth.

Of course right after they cross the stage, there is the getting them off safely to college, supporting them should they pledge a sorority or fraternity, or maybe helping them come up with ideas for their campaign slogans as they run for student government president. Maybe it's getting them into a trade school for graphic arts, enrolling them in cosmetology school, or helping them set up an internship with a fashion magazine.

They will come to you when they meet the person they want to marry, dig in your pockets when they are planning their wedding, and you'll be at the hospital, camera in hand, when your son or daughter and their spouse welcome your first grandchild into the world.

There to celebrate all of these accomplishments will be your child's blended family. The family that may not have been put together by choice, but who decided to work together to lead their children down the right path, and avoid the road they had to travel.

A self-sacrificing plan that assured that they come out of the challenging situation whole, complete, and lacking nothing.

Blend Well

Resources

Blended Families
www.theblendedfamilysurvivalguide.com

Opening a Child Support Case (Georgia)
Georgia Fatherhood Program
http://www.georgia.gov
http://www.cse.dhr.state.ga.us/apply.html - application

Resources for Single moms
www.singlemom.com

Resources for Fathers
www.fatherhood.org
www.fathers.com

Family & Marriage Counseling Directory
http://family-marriage-counseling.com/

World Law Direct
ttp://www.worldlawdirect.com/forum/law-wiki/5951-law-wiki.html

Divorce Forms & Papers
http://www.edivorcepapers.com